MILLION DOLLAR LAUNCH

Other Works by Alan Weiss

Alan Weiss on Consulting (interviewed by Chad Barr, Linda Henman, Aviv Shahar)
Best Laid Plans (originally *Making It Work*)
Getting Started in Consulting (also in Chinese)
Good Enough Isn't Enough (also in Spanish)
Great Consulting Challenges
How to Acquire Clients
How to Establish a Unique Brand in the Consulting Profession
How to Market, Brand, and Sell Professional Services
How to Sell New Business and Expand Existing Business
How to Write a Proposal That's Accepted Every Time
Life Balance
Managing for Peak Performance (also in German)
Million Dollar Business
Million Dollar Coaching (also in Portuguese)
Million Dollar Consulting (also in Portuguese, Russian, Polish, Chinese, Korean, and Arabic)
Million Dollar Consulting Proposals
Million Dollar Consulting® Toolkit
Million Dollar Referrals
Million Dollar Speaking (also in Chinese and Portuguese)
Million Dollar Web Presence (with Chad Barr)
Money Talks (also in Chinese)
Organizational Consulting
Our Emperors Have No Clothes
Process Consulting
The Consulting Bible
The Global Consultant (with Omar Kahn)
The Great Big Book of Process Visuals
The Innovation Formula (with Mike Robert; also in German, Italian)
The Son of the Great Big Book of Process Visuals
The Talent Advantage (with Nancy MacKay)
The Ultimate Consultant
The Unofficial Guide to Power Management
The Power of Strategic Commitment (with Josh Leibner and Gershon Mader)
Thrive!
Value Based Fees
Who's Got Your Back? (with Omar Kahn)

MILLION DOLLAR LAUNCH

HOW TO KICK-START A SUCCESSFUL CONSULTING PRACTICE IN 90 DAYS

ALAN WEISS, PhD

New York   Chicago   San Francisco   Athens   London
Madrid   Mexico City   Milan   New Delhi
Singapore   Sydney   Toronto

1 2 3 4 5 6 7 8 9 0   QFR/QFR   1 2 0 9 8 7 6 5 4

ISBN   978-0-07-182634-1
MHID   0-07-182634-3

e-ISBN   978-0-07-182355-5
e-MHID   0-07-182355-7

McGraw-Hill Education books are available at special quantity discounts to use as premiums and sales promotions or for use in corporate training programs. To contact a representative, please visit the Contact Us pages at www.mhprofessional.com.

For the first time as a team:
Buddy Beagle
Bentley, the white German shepherd

Contents

PROLOGUE   xi

INTRODUCTION   xiii

PART I

THE FIRST 30 DAYS

1 Departing and Starting   3

Maintaining Bridges   3

Consolidating Contacts   7

Building the Bank   10

Finding a Home   13

Gathering Support   17

2 Setting Up Shop   21

Legal Beagles   21

Equipment and Supplies   24

Local Finances and Design   28

Scheduling Your Time   31

Accepting (and Ignoring) Advice   35

3   Welcome to the Marketing Business   **39**

Creating Brands   39

Finding Your Value Proposition   43

Moving from Avocation to Occupation   46

Identifying Your Sweet Spot   49

Blowing Your Own Horn   52

Million Dollar Consulting® Market Gravity   56

Summary of The First 30 Days   59

Part I Review   **61**

PART II

THE SECOND 30 DAYS

4   Close Encounters of the Client Kind   **73**

Finding that Elusive and Important Number One   73

Marketing for Free   76

Creating Pipelines   80

Creating and Qualifying Leads   82

The Million Dollar Consulting® Qualifying System
  Template   83

Getting Paid   86

5   Creating Your Digital Empire   **91**

The Internet Upsides and Downsides   91

How to Create and Exploit a Great Blog   94

The Truth about Social Media   97

The Real Estate of Your Website   100

When High Touch Trumps High Tech   104

6 Pursuing the Ideal Prospect   **109**

The Market Value Bell Curve   109

Streams You Enter and Streams You Create   112

Delivering While Marketing, Marketing While
    Delivering   115

Why Any Partnership Will Work Against You   119

Wholesale and Retail   122

Part II Review   **125**

PART III

THE THIRD 30 DAYS

7 Diversifying Your Approaches   **143**

The Million Dollar Consulting® Accelerant Curve   143

Taking the Role of Expert, Not Consultant   146

Building Your Name as a Brand (Yes, Already)   149

Broadcasting the Array of Your Services   152

Going Viral   156

8 Creating Passive Income   **159**

Web-Based Products and Services   159

Subscription Services   162

Hard-Copy Value in a Digital World   166

Remote Coaching   169

9 Close to Home: Life Balance   **173**

Drawing People to You   173

Maximizing Vacations   176

Utilizing Your Support Structure   180

Investing Wisely   183

Procuring Ongoing Help   186

Part III Review   **191**

EPILOGUE: BEYOND THE FIRST 90 DAYS

**10   The Vital Need to Build and Nurture
      Self-Esteem**   **205**

Self-Talk   205

Support Groups Outside the Home   208

Building Efficacy   212

The Success Loop   215

Avoiding the Roller Coaster but Keeping the Thrill   218

APPENDIX   223

ACKNOWLEDGMENTS   237

INDEX   239

Prologue

In 1985, I was fired.

I had been asked to take over a boutique consulting firm in Providence, Rhode Island, the year before, so my wife and our nine- and ten-year-old children moved up from New Jersey. I had little in the way of savings, a new mortgage, private school tuition, and credit card debt. The Chicago-based owner of the firm—he owned 40 companies—and I didn't get along well at all, and he fired me in the Admirals Club of O'Hare Airport with his entourage at his side, and offered a grudging four months of severance.

I tell you this because, occasionally, someone supposes that I never had to start my own firm or that I've always had major assets.

Believe me, I know *exactly* what it's like to launch a business, except that I did so in a lousy economy, with no Internet, in a state where we had few contacts, and with no reserve or cushion.

I think it's important that you know this. I think it's also important that you know that I operate a multimillion-dollar business from my home today. I tell you that not to boast, but to express what's clearly possible for you. I could be making more than I do, but I have no need to, because, as you'll learn throughout this book, wealth is discretionary time and money is merely the fuel for it.

My initial reaction to being fired was anger. Most people either become angry or become distraught. The latter does nothing but make the situation worse. The former provides fuel for growth. I didn't want revenge—I didn't care about the moron who fired me—I wanted success for myself and my family. I knew that success could come only through independence and not dependence. You are reading this book because you are contemplating or actively pursuing the same dynamic.

In my case, I started getting on airplanes and flying to see prospects, whom I carefully qualified, since the airfare was on my own credit card. I spoke and wrote wherever I could—for free or for a fee—because these were my strengths and I wanted to build on them. I wasn't a good networker, there was no World Wide Web, and I hated cold calling and direct mail. So I went with my strengths and never let up.

My intention here is to enable you to do the same, but with a structure I didn't have at the outset and later found out I had created. Most recently, I've focused on making people more successful during their careers, but I asked myself—and my publisher—why this couldn't be supercharged for people who were launching their new careers.

Thus, I've tried to cull my mistakes—too many brochures and listings, for example—and focus on my successes—getting in front of buyers, building a brand—to streamline the process for you. In my first year on my own, I made $67,000. That would be roughly $130,000 today, or about $11,000 per month. My second year, I made $127,000, or about a quarter of a million in today's money: $20,000 per month.

But today you have access to a global market; you can interact with great influence with others remotely; it's far easier to identify and find ideal buyers; you can work concurrently in the corporate (wholesale) and consumer (retail) markets; and leverage and scalability are far easier and more effective than ever before.

As you read on, bear in mind that I've been there and done that, and have the T-shirt. You're hearing from a kindred spirit. I always ask myself when someone wants to achieve a new goal: "Has anyone, anywhere, at any time accomplished this?" If so, the chances are others can as well.

Believe me, you can do it.

Introduction

I've been working with entrepreneurs for a quarter of a century, particularly those who provide professional services on both a wholesale (corporate) and retail (consumer) basis. The conventional wisdom for a start-up was to try to assemble six-to-twelve months of average living expenses as a buffer against the usual long march toward business.

I found that some of my clients were able to close new business within one month and quite a few within three months. Some were never able to close new business, and no amount of bank reserves would be sufficient for the remainder of their lives.

As I write this in an unmistakably improving economy in the United States—despite Washington gridlock—and situationally improving economies around the world (Germany, Brazil, India, China, et al.), there is a cadre of people who want to build their own entrepreneurial businesses but for whom gathering the archetypical cash reserve would represent an insurmountable obstacle. These are recent grads, ex-military, retired, downsized, those fed up with corporate insecurity and bureaucracy, women returning to the workforce, and so on.

I felt that I could distill the finest attributes and learnable skills of those who have hit the ground running and closed business quickly in one place. Fortunately, so did my publisher.

Consequently, you have in the following pages more than a guide or direction. You have *specific techniques and steps* that will take you from a desire to be your own boss to a launch with escape velocity and ongoing acceleration. You won't hit the ground running because my intention is that you don't even hit the ground.

The most important aspect of the approaches I've assembled is not to fight them. Don't say "It won't work for me" or "I can't do that." Successful people never talk that way. They say "I have to figure out how to make that work for me" and "I can do that even better!"

The best way to use this book is to read it through entirely, then go back to the first chapter and begin the sequence. An understanding of the entire process will be of immense help as you go through the early steps.

I've provided scripts at the conclusions of each segment within the chapters. Sometimes these are intended for use with other people, and sometimes for yourself—your own self-talk. These are meant to give you some idea of how to verbalize, and thereby better understand, the concepts.

I've also provided major reviews after each of the 30-day segments. These reviews delve deeper into some aspects of the chapters. I don't want to overwhelm you with information in your first reading, so you may choose to ignore the reviews the first time around. Later, you may want to read them carefully for more depth. I leave the option to you as an additional learning tool when most appropriate.

They call me "the rock star of consulting." I've made millions for my coaching clients all over the world. Turn the page and join the flight.

MILLION DOLLAR LAUNCH

PART I
THE FIRST 30 DAYS

1

DEPARTING AND STARTING

OVERVIEW

Using the momentum of former jobs, contacts, and expertise in professional and private relationships to create early resources.

The child who innocently asks where he came from often receives an awkward explication on the need for love, its expression, the origins of life, and the beauty of it all. But the kid found out that his friend was from Bayonne and simply wondered where his family had been before coming to Asbury Park.

We're all from somewhere. In this business, our roots, previous connections, and acquaintances are to be highly valued.

MAINTAINING BRIDGES

It's crazy to burn bridges, but simply refraining from arson is insufficient. You need to maintain them, prevent rust and disrepair, and keep them sufficient for heavy traffic.

There is a tendency today to conduct the "grand resignation" (thanks to YouTube), where an aggrieved employee hires a marching band and parades through the halls singing of his quitting the galleys and leaving the Roman Navy. This is not someone who's going to garner any future goodwill from that former employer.

If you seek to make money quickly on your own, your best sources are those you already know. In fact, here's our first launch lesson.

Launch Lesson

Try to leave your current employer, if you have one, with a contract to provide the same services you're currently providing but as a consultant, not an employee.

When you decide to go out on your own, *be very nice to people.* This is not the time to settle scores or throw rocks. This includes:

- Current and past employers
- School faculty, deans, and administrators
- Social connections
- Civic connections
- Trade and professional association members
- Church and religious connections
- Professional connections (doctors, attorneys, accountants, etc.)
- Family, both immediate and extended

I've spoken to too many people who insulted their Uncle Harry once too often at the holidays, when it was irrelevant that Prudential Insurance thought enough of him to make him a senior vice president, one who could now provide referrals to peers and colleagues throughout the industry—if they were still talking to each other.

It's vital that you act as the offense in a military campaign. The defenders are usually trying to blow up bridges so the assaulters can't utilize them and the assaulters are trying to save them to speed their troops into new territory. It's no small irony that the new territory is the old territory, viewed far differently.

You will need everyone possible to help you get business in the first 90 days, *and you can't be sure who will be instrumental at the outset.* Thus, you have to be mindful of treating everyone well and maintaining contact. We'll talk about those contacts and the management there in the next section of this chapter, but for now bear in mind:

> **Contact:** Someone who remembers you, thinks well of you, and will take your call or respond to your e-mail with an inclination to be of help to you without expecting immediate reciprocity.

A contact is not simply a name on a mailing list or in a phone book. For our purposes, a contact is someone who will listen, talk, and help in those instances in which they can. Since you can't be sure exactly who that will be because your business is so new (and different from your former relationships), you can't afford to discriminate: *Everyone* is important at this point.

These bridges provide immediate momentum. Most—yes, *most*—people who launch their own businesses as solo practitioners sit by the phone and expect it to ring (or wait for the blue thing in their ear to buzz). They assume their e-mail will bring them riches, but they only get requests to maximize their search engine optimization (SEO) from some stranger in India who is even more at a loss than they are.

Here are some guidelines for maintaining and improving bridges (and even building them where none existed):

1. Be honest with former employers. Give them fair notice when you leave. Don't try to compete with them. Don't attempt to steal clients (or pencils or computers) from them.

2. Be modest with current peers and colleagues. Don't depart with "Sucker, I'm out of this dungeon and you're going to rot!" Point out that it was a hard decision and you hope to be up to the challenge.

3. For those who are of high potential in all likelihood (by position, those they know, sources of advice, and so on), make a date to talk in the future. Get a time and date certain on which to contact them, and update them on your progress and get their advice and referrals.

4. Ask for referrals before you depart: "You know some people over at your former company. Would you be willing to introduce me to them, or allow me to use your name when I approach them?"

5. Ask permission to send them information. Once you have your web presence, collateral, and your act together, send them some information to keep yourself visible. You want to remain on people's minds.

6. Get rid of bridge toll collectors. Respond to people immediately. Make yourself accessible and available. Ensure that they have your cell phone and home numbers. (Even today, I return *all* phone calls within 90 minutes during business hours. I suggest your initial business hours should be 8 a.m. to 8 p.m.)

If you handle this well, you'll have some excellent ongoing sources of business, referrals, and advice. Now you have to manage them.

Script

Don't call yourself a coach, a consultant, a speaker, or a trainer (or anything else). Call yourself an expert. Your expertise can be delivered in numerous ways (coaching, speaking, consulting, and so forth), but you don't want to arbitrarily box yourself into what may be unattractive packaging for some.

Focus on your value proposition, which should be a business outcome for the buyer; never focus on your methodology. If you're a sales expert, for example, don't talk about your sales training sessions. Instead:

My expertise is in dramatically decreasing closing times while cutting the costs of acquisition.

Now try creating yours: Business outcomes, stated as your expertise and appealing to the buyer:

_____

_____

CONSOLIDATING CONTACTS

Now that you have bridges—and you may still be in your job or avocation, or just beginning your own practice without a business card yet printed—you need to consolidate your contacts.

I'm often asked, "What would you have done differently if you were starting over today?" My answer is simple: Accumulate and exploit names.

Even though the technology of my nascent company was primitive (a multiline phone was a huge deal), I could easily have done a far better job of recording and identifying these dramatically important resources. And I should have known better. In my first consulting job for a firm in Princeton, I worked with a guy in his early thirties who had graduated from Harvard. He had a black book, about 5 × 8, in which was listed everyone he had gone to school with, worked with, met, helped, been helped by, or run into in the supermarket.

He was constantly erasing and correcting entries in the dog-eared pages (in the seventies, technology was a push-button phone). But if the company's owner said he was going to be in New York and wanted to meet someone in city government, or the nonprofit arena, or insurance, my friend had several names who would always be responsive to a call. He was worth his upkeep merely because of his seemingly infinite contacts, which continued to grow exponentially.

Launch Lesson

Keep every name, because you never know who will prove to be useful as a client, recommender, referral source, advisor, or free meal. You can always eliminate names, but you can never recreate those you've lost.

Here's the best way to organize your names on any decent computer platform:

1. Keep two lists, one alphabetical and another by category, for quick discovery.

2. Include name, address, e-mail, phone, website (if applicable), and a notes section. I recommend a simple application such as FileMaker Pro.

3. Create categories in the second list:
   - Client
   - Prospect
   - Reference Source
   - Advisor
   - Bankers and Credit
   - Professionals
   - Media and PR

It's fine to have overlap in these areas, because the point is to find *categories of people* quickly. Thus:

Clients: Those who are buyers and can send or authorize checks.

Prospects: Those who are presumed to be future buyers.

Reference sources: People who will serve as a reference or provide a testimonial.

Advisor: Those to whom you turn for specialized advice, such as attorneys, CPAs, coaches, designers, and so on.

Bankers and credit: Those who can provide loans and credit support.

Professionals: Doctors, lawyers, accountants, and so forth (these people are very useful for referral business).

Media and PR: Local, national, global editors, talk show producers, bloggers, reviewers, and others who can endorse you as a third party and reach large numbers of people.

You can modify these any way you wish and, given your particular expertise and markets, may continually do so as your practice grows. But this is a good start, and can be completed within the first few days of your launch. That's why bridges are so important.

Here's a very important, often ignored fact: You never know where your next hit is coming from. To this day, I'm never sure whether a newsletter, speech, blog post, networking event, product, video, or referral will result in my next piece of business. And I don't care. The more initial contacts you capture and build upon, the higher the chances that you'll have early initial sales. Some people can walk away from an employer with a consulting contract, which is as fast as you can do it. But many obtain sales in the first 30 days by assiduously creating and utilizing a comprehensive contact list.

One case in point: You often refer people to your doctor or attorney as a courtesy, believing you're helping all parties involved. But doctors and attorneys rarely reciprocate, not out of malice *but because they don't know what your value is to others.* A dentist may well have a patient in the chair who is complaining about how hard it is to find a good coach. That dentist needs to know you are a superb coach.

Therefore, these contacts are the early seeding to make sure the crop grows well and can sustain you nutritionally. You'll want to let everyone know that you're now on your own, what your value is, and how to contact you. That sounds simple, but most people starting new practices ignore it and instead focus on computer software or staring at the phone.

Finally, as you build your contact list, use a simple priority (high, medium, low) to indicate relative importance in each category. (Don't get complicated with numbers.) A *high* indicates a highly reliable, high potential source, *medium* is someone who may prove helpful under certain conditions, and *low* is unknown or rarely of help.

Script

Practice what you'll say when you reach out to people so that it's natural and win/win/win. Example:

I've launched my own practice using my expertise to help clients achieve high-potential referrals daily to dramatically increase their market share. I'd like your advice about to whom you think I should be presenting my ideas, and if you'd be kind enough to introduce me. I'd be eager to know how I can be of help with your referrals as well.

BUILDING THE BANK

There are two primary—perhaps even *exclusive*—causes of failure in the first three months:

1. Relationship and support issues
2. Financial issues

We'll address the first at the conclusion of this chapter because it tends to be the foundation (or lack thereof) for all else, so let's focus on the monetary obstacles here.

Henry Ford (also attributed to Vince Lombardi) observed that "Obstacles are those things you see when you take your eyes off the goal." We tend to view our financial resources as an off/on switch—either we have them or we don't. But, in fact, finances are really more like a rheostat that can be adjusted.

No one I have ever mentored or coached—and we're talking about thousands of people over nearly three decades—has ever lost their home, been thrown out of their apartment, starved to death, or lacked for clothing. No one. There have been times for many, including me, when we realized we would have to incur debt, delay payments, tone down lifestyles, and so on. But those are simply intelligent tactics (and episodes that almost always enormously add to our growth and resilience).

You should have these sources of financial support at the time you launch your practice, whether planned or forced due to circumstances:

- Money in the bank
- Savings and IRA accounts
- Investment and securities
- Home equity
- Credit lines and credit cards
- Loan potential
- Family resources
- Expenses that can be reduced
- Items that can be sold
- New client business

Early in my career, I jotted down the amounts available if I maximized all of these options, just in theory. The total, in the late eighties, was $440,000. At the time, our bank account had exactly $1,250!

I'm not advocating excessive debt or a haphazard approach to finances. But I am telling you that you have more resources than you might imagine, and if you're serious and passionate about your new career and gaining traction quickly, then borrowing from a 401(k) or relying on a spouse's income or taking a home equity loan is intelligent, not anathema.

Take a moment and go through my exercise. If you had to do so, how much cash could you accumulate if you maximized all of the options above:

$\$$_____

Remember, the plan is to have income flowing in 90 days, so you're not going to require anything but a small fraction of that amount.

> ### Launch Lesson
> *In the first few days, satisfy yourself that the money is there in reality or in virtuality, and stop worrying about it. Focus your talents on launching your practice, not preserving dollars, and make sure your family and loved ones understand this.*

Make the time to visit your banker or financial advisor to prepare them for the fact that you may need some short-term credit. Do *not* listen to them about the "folly" of your entrepreneurial goals—they are stuck in nine-to-five jobs and won't appreciate (or will be envious of) your intended freedom. But do prepare them, and have them ready to provide advice and resources.*

Once you realize that there is money available or at least accessible, and that debt is a valid tactic in the short term to prime your launch, you can stop worrying about the mortgage and rent. I've had many clients tell me, "It finally happened. I exhausted my credit lines and missed a few payments, but I got through it. Here I am, better than ever, and now I can handle any kind of difficulty."

---

* Obviously, if you are planning your new career in advance, you can secure credit that much more easily and have it available. It's harder to do when you're thrust into this because of downsizing or other harsh measures. But understand this: Because of such exigencies, it's always a good idea to keep minimal credit-card balances and a healthy credit score.

You'll need a solid financial advisor—not an investment advisor—who can help with managing your money and debt, *and who can reassure family members as well, if they have concerns.*

You'll need a banking relationship if you don't already have one—that is, high-level contacts in the bank—so move all your assets to one bank, show that you're a good and high-potential customer, and find an officer who is willing to work with you on equity lines, loans, and so on.

You'll need a good insurance agent for the following (this won't come from your family agent):

- Errors and omissions insurance, commonly called malpractice insurance. Many companies demand this coverage before they will hire you. This protects against damages for "bad advice."

- Liability insurance, which covers you in case someone trips over a projector cord in a room in which you're presenting.

Everything that precedes you can accomplish before you formally launch or in the first couple of days. You need to get all of this behind you.

Script

I'm starting a new consulting (design, architecture, accounting) practice, and I may need some short-term financing to help with my initial marketing. I have solid credentials and clearly defined prospects whom I've already started to visit. What options can you provide in the event I need them?*

FINDING A HOME

You have two primary choices for work location: in your home or outside of it. This is not as simple as it seems. You can't merely flip a coin.

---

* Note how much more powerful this is if you can also say, apropos of our earlier discussion, "And I already have a signed contract from my former employer, which I've begun working on and am being paid for."

When I was fired in 1985, my wife was entirely supportive of my plans to go out on my own, though she questioned why I wanted to find an office to rent.

"I have a new practice."

"Yes, but why do you need an office."

"I have no office anymore, so I need a place to work."

"Yes, but why an office?"

"Okay, you clearly have a point you want to make."

"You're going to go see people, they aren't coming to you. Why spend money on an office now? If you find that you need one, you can always get one at any time."

Today, people *do* come to me, and at very high fees. But I still don't have an office. And in the first 17 years of my solo practice, I calculated that with rent, utilities, insurance, repairs, and part-time help, I would have spent about $450,000. That is almost exactly the amount I invested in private schools for my two kids, from kindergarten through an undergraduate degree. Not having an office paid for their tuition, which I paid for out of cash flow.

That's the importance of this decision. Working at home can be a blessing in terms of convenience and support, or a curse in terms of distraction and interruptions.

Here's what you need for a productive, comfortable office environment at home:

- A room with a door that is relatively soundproof. A part of a room or a curtain partition will not suffice.

- Proper wiring: You'll need Internet access and at least a two-line phone in your office. (No, a cell won't be sufficient. You need both the house line and your business line to ring in there.) You'll need enough outlets for chargers and printers and so forth.

- Proper ventilation: air-conditioning and heat and healthy air circulation.

- Proper lighting: at least one window with exposure to natural light is required.

- Proper space: you'll need some paper file space, despite the digital age, and room for a computer, printer, postage meter, supplies, and the like.

- Agreement: Your spouse or significant other, children, and pets will have to stop at the closed door and not barge in. You'll need rules, such as knocking and no loud noises in the hall outside.

My office, which I've used for 29 years, is the smallest bedroom in the house. It has a large window overlooking the backyard, where I can watch the dogs, and a nearby bathroom. I've had it redesigned twice, as technology has advanced and my tastes changed, and it's perfect for my needs.

You'll have to have the discipline *not* to run out and play fetch with the dogs or chat with the kids, and the courage to tell your significant other that the latest household issues and chores will have to wait.

Launch Lesson

If you have basic privacy, and you can apply discipline, you're far better off working at home for convenience, support, economy, and flexibility. But those are big ifs.

If you choose not to—or can't—work at home, you have external options:

- In many cases, your attorney, accountant, or other professional acquaintances will have extra office space they can rent to you inexpensively. (And if you work at home but need meeting space at times, you can ask for this favor.) You'll often have the use with your rental of the central receptionist, conference room, copier, fax, and so on.

- There are shared suites in many cities where you can rent space full-time or part-time. You will usually share central services with other tenants. This gives you a formal address at which to receive mail and, usually, a conference area. One of my clients, a $5 million consultancy with 20 people, used this arrangement in Midtown Manhattan until they outgrew it and rented formal offices downtown.

- You can rent your own place. Be careful, because there will inevitably be a lease committing you to an extended period, and you'll have utilities, insurance, and maintenance to consider. You'll also probably have to furnish the place, especially if you might host a visiting client at times. Ideally, the office should have plenty of parking, be within a 30-minute commute, and not force you to take rush-hour, heavily used roads (even though you can make your own hours). There should be a security system, and you should be able to change the locks.

Before you begin, or in the first week, make a careful decision about where your new home will be. If you can work at home under the conditions I described, you're probably better off. As my wife suggested, you can always move out later.

Script

This is new for all of us, but I need privacy to work effectively, especially because clients might not find background noise from kids and dogs amusing! Can we agree on some simple rules to help me in my work?*

---

* The Great Dog Trotsky belched into a speakerphone once, prompting my client to ask, "What on earth was that? Are you okay?"

GATHERING SUPPORT

The most important aspect of your launch and quick success is your support system. For many, this will be family, but not for all. For some, it may be colleagues, a professional community, friends, or others. For some, it may be the combination of all of these people.

The key is to bring your support system into your new world. You should create transparency and candor. A truly supportive person will tell you when you're wrong and when you're right, in their judgment; he or she will describe why something is your fault or someone else's; people who care about you will not lie to you, especially when they recognize the vital importance of your endeavor.

Here is what I advise for a solid support system, particularly one that will enhance and not threaten existing relationships. (I've seen husbands and wives turn on each other when one doesn't truly understand what the other is trying to create.)

1. Be candid about why you're doing this. If you were fired, say so. I used to brag about it. ("I'm the only person you'll ever meet who was fired by someone wearing a cape!") Don't lie or create stories. "I was downsized. It wasn't fair, but here I am."

2. Explain the value you are creating for others and how it will generate business. "My expertise is in financial compliance, and I'll be offering best-practice audits that will enable senior management to take the temperature of their fiscal health quickly. My intent is to charge $10,000 for two days of work and to land two such clients every month."

3. Ask for help and referrals. "Where do you think I should be promoting this, and whom do we know to approach with it?"

4. Either persuade or dismiss the energy suckers and cynics. "I know you're having a hard time understanding such a radical transition, but all I ask is that you support and help for 90 days and you'll be

seeing dramatic results." *Or:* "This is not a time when I can absorb negativity, so if you can't support me, let's remove this as a subject between us," or "Let's not meet again for another 90 days."

5. It's a *must* that your spouse be with you. You need to convince your partner to be at least patient and, preferably, wildly supportive. Sometimes they can take part in the venture: doing the books, handling correspondence and messages, or researching prospects.

> ### Launch Lesson
> *Ideally, line up your support in advance if you're planning a future launch date. If the launch is forced upon you, get this done quickly. Emotional support is more important in your success than software or bankers.*

6. Talk about your day, your plans, your wins, and your losses publicly: at the dinner table or wherever appropriate. Just because you have an office at home doesn't mean you should act like a boarder. Share with your family what's happening to get feedback and keep them apprised.

7. Hold formal or informal meetings with nonfamily support group members so that they, too, can offer advice and remain knowledgeable about your business.

8. If necessary—if your spouse or significant other is continually negative, scared, or sarcastic—seek counseling. These reactions are almost always the sign of deeper problems in the relationship, not based solely on your new venture, but they will kill the new venture nonetheless. Don't live with this, because 99 percent of the time it will be fatal to your business.

Script

Sweetheart, I need your help. I can help you understand my business, but more important, you understand me. These can be scary times or exciting times, depending on our joint outlook. I need you to let me know when you think I'm doing the right thing or the wrong thing, and I need to be comfortable asking for your help with decisions and risks. If we can do this together, we're going to be happier than ever.

SETTING UP SHOP

OVERVIEW

The basics with which to begin and the distractions
to avoid. You can always fine-tune later.

There are basic necessities, desirable items, and complete wastes of time and money. Start simple for two reasons. First, you have limited money to invest. Second, you have limited time to invest, which should be directed to the stage and not backstage.

LEGAL BEAGLES

You may well have an estate attorney and/or someone who closed on your house or has helped with some local disputes. You will need a corporation attorney who can help incorporate your business in some form immediately. You generally do *not* want a DBA (doing business as) because it looks unprofessional and lacks certain advantages. Nor, as of this writing, is a chapter C company attractive any longer—this is what most major corporations use—because the benefits and deductions unique to that configuration have disappeared.

This leaves either a subchapter S or an LLC (limited liability corporation). Your attorney, with your accountant, can tell you which is best under your state's laws. Both forms offer legitimate business deductions but flow through your personal tax return. I had a $1.5 billion client, closely held, that used subchapter S.

Launch Lessons

Don't have your cousin Louie take care of your legal matters, even if he only demands food as compensation. Find a pro and expect to pay about $350 an hour, depending upon where you reside.

Eventually, you'll need an IP (intellectual property) attorney, who will handle copyright and trademark matters. You'll also need access to a litigator although, like a fire extinguisher, you'll hope to never have to turn it on. In almost every case, your mortgage or estate attorney *cannot* handle these issues, though another partner in the firm might be right for you.

Be very careful about attribution. As a good learner and student, you may well read a great deal about your area of passion and expertise. But take pains not to advertently or inadvertently use others' property. When in doubt, attribute. More importantly, develop your own original ideas, and place them in the public forum continually.

You read that correctly. Don't hide your intellectual property as though it were gold and others will steal it. You can put your money under your mattress and no one might find it, but it won't earn you a cent, either. You have to invest your ideas in public so that others can identify them as yours and seek you out to obtain more.

As a rule, create proposals that are also a means of consummating the deal (see the appendix for a proposal example). You *do not* want an attorney to draw up your proposals, which they will attempt to make risk-free, totally in your favor, and archly conservative. When that happens, the document goes to your prospect's legal department, which is larger than yours (!) and has even more of a need to justify its existence. Before you know it, a simple three-page proposal will become a 42-page bloblike monster, with enough "third parties shall hold harmlesses" to make you think you're negotiating to purchase the State of Vermont.

Here are the things your attorney(s) should do for you:

1. Assist as needed in incorporation that best meets your needs.

2. Apply for trademark and service mark protection and monitor progress through registration approval.

3. Send warning letters when someone has directly copied from you without attribution.

4. Review contracts sent to you, e.g., from government agencies, hotels where you may hold workshops, subcontracting work from larger companies, and so on.

5. Refer prospects to you from their client base and contacts in the community.

6. Apprise you of any changes in the laws or pending legislation that may affect your business.

7. Ensure you are in compliance with federal and state regulations, i.e., filing annual reports.

8. Form corporate bylaws.*

---

*These can be vital, such as stipulating that all noninsured medical expenses are paid for by the corporation, or that directors' fees may be paid, or that an annual meeting is to be held at corporate expense.

Here is what you should *not* ask of or expect from your attorney:

1. Serving as an advisor to you on nonlegal matters. Lawyers are clueless about billing (they use time units), don't understand marketing, and are entirely risk-averse. That's why they're lawyers.

2. Financial advice of any kind.

3. Services outside of their specialty. Generally, litigation, contract law, and trademark work are done by different people.

It's best to consult with your attorney as soon as you've made the decision to go out on your own. This way you won't do something foolish through ignorance that you'll have to reverse.

> **Script**
>
> *John, I've made the decision to become a solo designer (consultant, speaker, architect), and I need your help in drafting my company's bylaws, setting up the LLC and registering it with the state, and exploring trademark protection for a few of my ideas. Can you and your partners help, and am I missing anything?*

EQUIPMENT AND SUPPLIES

I talked earlier about a private space in your home, a shared space with a professional provider, or a rented space. No matter where you are, here's what you need to put in it *at the outset*. Later on, after money is coming in, you can refine this to your heart's content.

> *Phone:* As of this writing, I still strongly suggest a landline phone. Find one with the following:
> - Two lines (one for your home line, one for your business line)

- Answering message capability (unless you forward to a service)
- Conference calling
- Wireless extensions (for other parts of the house)
- Speed dial and memory
- Headphone-capable

Be careful: If you purchase a package or bundle from your Internet provider, in the event of a power outage or cable problem, you can find yourself concurrently without television, landline phone, cell phone, and computer service.

A toll-free number is not terribly important today, but if you get one, make sure it works internationally so you don't inadvertently irritate overseas prospects who see the number on your site and try to call.

You'll also need a fax number—a third line—if you anticipate faxes—they are still used by many overseas—and your computer can't handle faxes or you prefer it doesn't. What you *don't* want is a common line that says to "wait for the beep" or take some other action to send a fax on the same number. Since you'll often want to answer your home phone in your office—or have a conference call with another party on that line—plan for three lines: home, office, and fax. One cell phone won't cut it.

Computer: Suit yourself. I use a desktop, laptop, and iPad. I do a lot of writing and I prefer a full, integrated keyboard. But an air book, mini, or some other device might well meet your own purposes, and these offerings change monthly. I would suggest software such as Dropbox and/or Evernote, so that what you place on one platform is immediately replicated on all platforms, which both makes work easier and serves as a backup.

Speaking of which, you don't need seven backup systems whereby you can emerge after nuclear calamity and do business on the moon. Use your judgment. Multiple hard drives and software solutions are time consuming and silly. Presumably, if you lost *all* of your records, your client would still call *you*!

Copier: I suggest a copier/printer/fax/scanner combination; they have really been perfected and require less of a footprint and are less expense. These work aids are a necessity, and combining them is the best way to move forward.

Credit card terminal: More and more clients are inclined to pay with credit cards on the wholesale (corporate) side, and almost everyone does on the retail (consumer) side. Go to your commercial bank, have them set up a relationship with MasterCard and Visa (and Discover, if you like), and then call American Express and have them tie into the same terminal. This is a minor expense, and you'll pay between 2. 5 and 3.5 percent for credit card purchases, but this is simply a cost of doing business. (You can also process credit cards on your computer or smartphone, or even automatically by a third-party source.)

Postage meter and scale: Going to the post office is a huge time dump. Use Pitney Bowes or another such service (such as stamps.com or endicia.com), lease at least a ten-pound scale and meter, and complete all your addressing and postage at your office. Don't stand in lines at the post office. Keep a supply of international customs forms and certified mail slips.

Along the same lines, keep both FedEx and UPS supplies (they're free), create an account with each, and have boxes and packages picked up at your place.

Furniture: A card table can always serve as a desk. Don't go into hock for furniture at the beginning. What you'll need is a desk with drawers, a couple of simple file cabinets, a comfortable chair, a visitor's chair, and some shelves or drawers for supplies. At the outset, you'll seldom see anyone except you in your office, so don't worry too much about amenities. I would suggest a radio, photos or art on the walls, and some sound-deadening features such as carpeting.

Launch Lesson

In whatever space you use, make it a happy place. Hang photos and art that you like, display awards and mementos, play music that you enjoy. The happier you are in your surroundings, no matter how simple, the more positive you'll be in your work.

Letterhead and such: You'll sometimes need to send hard-copy correspondence, and business cards are still useful so that people can retain your contact information. Put your company name and logo and contact numbers on a business card, letterhead, envelopes, and labels. Use a designer to help you acquire a professional but inexpensive look.

Duplicate all of this electronically so that you can use it in your e-mail signature file, proposals sent over the web, and so on.

Storage: You're going to have to keep tax data, client records, expense reports, income statements, and related business material for a minimum of five years and often longer. Even your computer files will have to be removed and stored on discs at some point to free up space.

You'll need either an area at home that is safe from heat, cold, and water, or a climate-controlled storage area outside of your home (these run about $150 or so a month). Keep close what you may need access to in your normal business, and store farther away what you would need only in the result of financial or legal inquiry.

> **Script**
> *What is the least expensive, most user-friendly equipment and arrangements that can efficiently produce these outcomes for me on a regular basis?*

LOCAL FINANCES AND DESIGN

You'll eventually need a variety of financial experts, because we all should plan for success:

- Bookkeeping
- Tax preparation
- Financial planning
- Business and personal credit

The only one that I want to mention during the first 90 days is the bookkeeping. If you want to bring business in the door rapidly, don't waste time doing things you can pay others a modest amount to do for you.

That means that Quicken and other software designed to "keep your books" and balance your accounts is not the way to go. Would you want your prospects to be relying on consulting software instead of hiring you, a legitimate expert?

I didn't think so.

Ask other entrepreneurs and small business owners in your area whom they would recommend. If you already have an accountant, he or she can almost always recommend a good bookkeeper. My current bookkeeper picks up the paperwork at my house once a month and delivers back to me a week or so later my checkbook reconciliations, general ledger, income and expense by category, comparisons against prior years, and a list of uncashed checks outstanding.

She does this for about $300 a month, and I'm running a complex, $3-million solo business as you read this. I know software would cost that $300 for eternal use, but what of the time I invest, the mistakes I'll inevitably make, and similar issues? Trust me, you can afford what will probably be $150 a month.

> ### Launch Lesson
> *Pay local venders quickly so that you have their priority time when you need it, but insist on pay for performance and intelligent work. One bookkeeper candidate told me she posted by hand, not computer, yet charged by the hour. "So you deliberately choose a slow method and penalize me for it?" I asked. She didn't get the job.*

There's a simple invoice sample in the appendix. Print these out on your computer or send them electronically on the letterhead we discussed earlier. If you don't already know him or her, make sure you introduce yourself to your local branch manager, and say hello whenever you visit. This will help tremendously if you want to avoid small charges and fees (e.g., being overdrawn) or if you need a brief bridge loan. Make sure you get overdraft protection on your business and personal accounts.

You'll also need a local designer. This is the person who would design your logo or letterhead, slides for presentations, booklets, client handouts, and even your website.

Graphics designers generally charge by the hour, so it's easy to give them a cap or maximum. Always ask for several versions or options, not a fait accompli. As with finance, it's actually much cheaper to have experts take care of this instead of trying to do it yourself under the false notion that you're saving money (while hemorrhaging time).

However, here's an even better way. Go to a local university or community college and advertise for an art student who'd like to make some extra money. You'll find extremely talented people who need the work and the substance on their résumé. You can usually strike quite a mutually beneficial deal for a reasonable fee (again, pay for performance).

Don't search for the perfect logo or design. In the first 90 days, you simply want to rely on a good, professional look you can always change later if you choose to. A designer will help you with fonts, colors,* size, white space, photos, artwork, graphs, and so on. I've changed logos and styles four times since I began my business. I may well change again. An example of my current logo appears below.

SUMMIT CONSULTING GROUP

Box 1009

East Greenwich, RI

02818-0964

Tel (401) 884-2778

Fax (401) 884-5068

Logo example

The logo is in my company colors, a mountain top to represent Summit, and my contact info. Nothing fancier than that, and it's consistent across my stationery and electronic media.

You're always better off with local suppliers and support (as opposed to Internet providers) because you can deal with them in person and

---

* For example, some people have a tendency to use pastels if they don't get professional advice, and those are not power shades or effective for presentations.

establish relationships. Your design and finance (and legal and other) support people can and should:

- Provide you with fast service
- Be highly responsive
- Provide very reasonable fees and charges
- Provide you with referrals

You won't get these things from virtual relationships, and any such cost savings aren't worth their loss.

As with the legal help, don't use Uncle Louie or your cousin's former college roommate who's looking for work. This is your business and your life, and the first three months may will determine long-term outcomes.

SCHEDULING YOUR TIME

Here is a basic guideline you must take to heart if you're going to close business within the first three months of launching your practice: *Time is not a resource, it's a priority.*

We all have 24 hours in a day; the question is how we allocate them. When people tell me that they would love to see their children play soccer but can't, what they're really saying is "I choose not to do so." Perhaps they have a good reason for not doing so—a business appointment that may pay for soccer and dance lessons for the rest of the year—but the fact is, they have made conscious choices.

This is one of the most important distinctions I've had to establish with corporate executives whom I've coached and entrepreneurs whom I've mentored. Time is about deciding on priorities and making conscious decisions about allocation and duration.

Consequently, you need both the means and the intent to allocate your time effectively from day one of your business. The intent should be to acquire clients as quickly as possible at maximum fees and with minimum labor intensity. The means include a daily accurate, infallible calendar.

> ### Launch Lesson
> *Paying down debt is as important as increasing income in most cases. Similarly, minimizing time involvement while meeting client objectives is as important as maximizing revenues. Excess time investment erodes your true wealth: discretionary time.*

My strong recommendation is that you use a physical calendar (e.g., a Filofax) to allocate your time. Electronic calendars are harder to access *and are impossible to use to see a full week, month, or year easily at one glance.* Since juxtaposition of events is as important as placement of events; you'll often need these kinds of overviews.

No matter what you use, schedule your day with realism and flexibility:

Realism: You're not going to write a complete book chapter in one session on a Tuesday morning.

Flexibility: The five pages you have scheduled for an hour may be interrupted by an urgent request or unexpected event, in which case you can slide it to Wednesday afternoon.

Here are three days in my physical calendar:

Monday, April 15

- Run workshop at hotel
- Have taxes sent in by certified mail
- Confirm dinner reservations for six tonight
- Call payroll service for paycheck
- Record podcast
- Check with printer on materials I've ordered

Tuesday, April 16

- 8:00 Skype call to Australia
- 9:00 Client phone call
- 10:00 Client phone call
- Write five pages of the book you're now reading
- Record podcast I didn't get to yesterday
- 4:30 Skype call to Japan

Wednesday, April 17

- 9:30 Skype call to UK
- Client conference call (one hour)
- 11:30 Haircut
- 1:00 Client call
- Write five pages of book you're now reading

During those three days, I managed a full workshop delivery, six client calls, 10 pages (about a half chapter) of writing, a recording that had to be flexibly rescheduled, and some administrative and personal stuff. I didn't schedule any calls on the workshop day (though I returned unscheduled calls during breaks and lunch).

During those three days, prior to 5 p.m., I probably also had five hours of completely free, discretionary time, during which I played fetch with Bentley, my German shepherd, read, worked on a model plane I'm building, gassed up the car, had lunch, posted on Twitter and my blog daily, and so on.

Here are the guidelines you should put on the wall of your office to gain this level of productivity right from the outset:

1. Success, not perfection. Don't try to make anything exactly correct. Simply strive for success and then move on. I could

improve this last sentence, but it wouldn't help you understand the point any better.

2. Say no. Don't take on other people's burdens at this sensitive part of your launch. Tell people your pick-my-brain fee is $5,000, and that will stop the requests. Remember, *you* allocate your time; you do not apportion it according to the needs of others. Even clients will change dates and times for you.

3. Keep your phone forwarded and return calls when you have the time planned or a window opens up. Don't feel constrained to be available to everyone all the time. Don't give too many people your cell-phone number.

4. Don't allow your computer or any other electronic device to interrupt you. Don't allow notifications of e-mails, texts, or software updates.

5. Check your e-mail three times a day at most: morning, noon, and the end of the business day.

6. Don't surf the Internet except on down time or weekends, and absolutely minimize the business hours you spend on any social media platform. These are *not* effective marketing tools to reach corporate buyers, no matter what self-appointed social-media marketing experts tell you. (Throw a rock down the street in Duluth and you'll hit four of these *experts*.)

Script

I'm sorry, but I can't help you for free, since this is my profession and that wouldn't be fair to my paying clients. There are free resources on my site, or you can choose to become a client. Therefore, I don't engage in casual lunches or pick-my-brain sessions.

ACCEPTING (AND IGNORING) ADVICE

By far the most insidious source of undermining you will experience as you launch your business is unsolicited advice. What I'm about to share with you may be the most important part of this entire book for many of you.

By all means, assemble a small brain trust of people you trust. This should *not* include your attorney or accountant—use them for their professional expertise, but both professions are notoriously conservative and involve poor business practices (i.e., hourly billing). Here's who you might involve in your inner circle:

- Your immediate family: spouse, significant other, grown children if they have business acumen, parents if they have business acumen.*

- Close friends, especially if they have created entrepreneurial businesses.

- A successful small-business founder who has done well and may agree to be your occasional mentor.

Five or so people are more than enough. A once-a-quarter group meeting and one-on-one phone calls as needed are appropriate. In your immediate family—your prime support group—you should be talking about your business daily. The conversation shouldn't be all-consuming, but you need to explain the challenges you face, victories and defeats endured, and advice you need.

All of the above constitutes *solicited* feedback, meaning you've sought input from those you've designated as appropriate and competent to provide it. It's the *unsolicited* feedback that can kill you.

There is a myth about feedback: The notion is that all of it is worthwhile to listen to and perhaps heed, and that the more you receive, the

---

* Just because parents lend you money doesn't mean they can effectively contribute business and marketing advice.

better off you'll be. I want to dispel that fairy tale right here, because this book is about making you successful quickly.

Most unsolicited feedback is for the *sender*, not the *recipient*. Most people do it for themselves. They offer free advice—with no personal consequence—for their own ego, for their public display of wisdom and superiority, and because they are threatened by someone like you taking bold and challenging actions they aren't willing to take.*

> **Launch Lesson**
>
> Feel free to say "No, thanks" when someone asks if they can offer feedback. Or listen politely and then forget about it. Otherwise, you're a ball in a Pachinko machine.

Psychologically, there is a dynamic called projection, which means that I extend my own experiences to you, as well as my own aspirations and fears. Thus, I may tell you that you won't be able to market to Fortune 500 companies because I was never able to myself. If you are able to do it, then that means you're better than I am at marketing, and I can't allow that in my belief universe.

Unsolicited feedback will not only chew up valuable time but will threaten to confuse and disrupt your plans. The idea is to get business in the bank within 90 days, and you don't have time to listen to random, unsupported, irrelevant advice, no matter what someone's (claimed) credentials.

I run a global forum for entrepreneurs (AlansForums.com), and I'm there daily, ensuring that no one is setting themselves up as an arbitrary expert and offering bad advice to newer people. You don't have that

---

* If you want a ski instructor, find someone who skis a few yards ahead of you on the slope, doing what you want to do, not someone who sits in the chalet sipping brandy telling you what to do the next morning.

filter or traffic cop; hence, I'm advocating a deliberately selected group of people on whom you can rely for solid advice, no matter how painful it may be at times.

What we've covered to this point should be attended to either before you officially launch, should you have that time and luxury, or in the first couple of days after launch, if you're suddenly in the wilderness (as I was, abruptly fired with very little severance). Don't make the mistake of regarding feedback and sources of help as omnipresent or omnipotent. They are neither. Be selective from the outset.

Sometimes what you *don't* do and *don't* accept is as important as what you deliberately do. In this case, you'll save yourself time and dozens of cul-de-sacs if you pay attention to whom you should pay attention.

Now that we're set up sufficiently to venture forth, let's get into the marketing business.

Script

While I appreciate your advice and interest in my new venture, I've secured some highly expert sources for coaching and I have to focus on a few key initiatives at this point. However, you can help me even more if you have names of people who may become clients/customers, and I'd be indebted if you could introduce me to them.

WELCOME TO THE MARKETING BUSINESS

No matter whether you are an architect, designer, consultant, coach, facilitator, trainer, insurance professional, realtor, or in any other professional service, make no mistake: You're really in the marketing business.

The problem is that few of us have a formal education in marketing, and those that do usually have an irrelevant and nonsensical one. If you say you dislike marketing yourself, then find another job working for someone who *can* market. Because your success in the first three months *and thereafter* will be in your ability to market yourself and your results.

CREATING BRANDS

You want to create a memorable persona quickly, so that people begin talking about you and mentioning you to others. The ultimate brand is your name (e.g., "Get me McKinsey"). But you can have multiple brands that can change as your career progresses.

At the outset, try to create something memorable. For example, I became the contrarian. I took an opposing view to conventional wisdom to stand out in a crowd of about 400,000 independent consultants when I was dumped on the sidewalk one day.

Thus, instead of teams, I announced that companies really had committees, and that team building didn't work. I pointed out that coaching and mentoring were two different things, the first proactive and the second reactive. I happily told everyone I could—in the midst of the hoopla around quality and Deming and Juran*—that quality circles were a waste of time, and most quality improvements were actually myths.

How did I do this? I wrote and spoke, wrote and spoke, wrote and spoke. I would write and speak anywhere for free, so long as I had audiences and could create some controversy. If you want to launch your business quickly and *successfully*, you can't be the 450,000th person talking about walking your talk or the importance of listening to customers. (Try talking the walk or ignoring customers.)

To this day, 25 years later, I'm still sometimes introduced at my keynote speeches as the contrarian, even though my name is widely known in my profession and I've written more books on consulting than anyone in history. That's the adhesion power of a strong brand.

A brand is a uniform representation of quality. That is, people can rely on a brand for consistency and constancy, whether it's McDonald's, Singapore Airlines, Dyson, or you! (See the brand pyramid on the facing page.)

Beyond the first three months, you can focus on brand building and brand equity. The latter occurs when people will pay merely based on the reputation of your brand/name. That's why you see Ferrari on watches, even though the car company knows nothing about making watches. They are cashing in on their brand equity.

For now, establish what your brand(s) should be, and broadcast that in your speaking, writing, conversations, networking, e-mail signature, and so on. Here are some questions to ask:

- How do I want to be known?
- What's my true expertise?

---

* The two gurus of the quality movement.

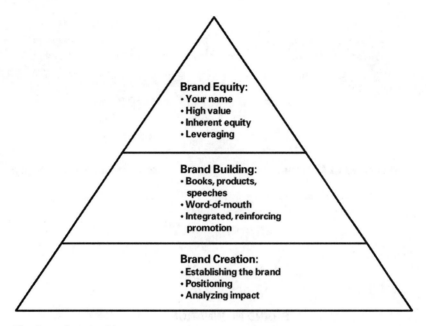

The brand pyramid

- What am I passionate about?
- What market need do I most want to satisfy?

If you are an expert in finance and want to help small business owners create valuable entities that will provide legacies for themselves and their families, perhaps you're the Legacy Creator.

If your expertise is in Internet marketing and you intend to help traditional businesses exploit sales in cyberspace, perhaps you're the Market Maven.

Perhaps you're a specialist in customer acquisition, retention, and referrals, and you'd like to be known as the Customer Asset Architect.

For now, don't worry about perfection, only movement. What is your inherent value and what's a memorable, appealing way to express it? Create three potential brands using the worksheet on the next page, and run them quickly by your brain trust. Find out which one resonates the most and begin with that.

> ### Launch Lesson
> *You need to stand out in the crowd. You can't be heard in a herd. Be bold and memorable in describing yourself. If you don't blow your own horn, there's no music.*

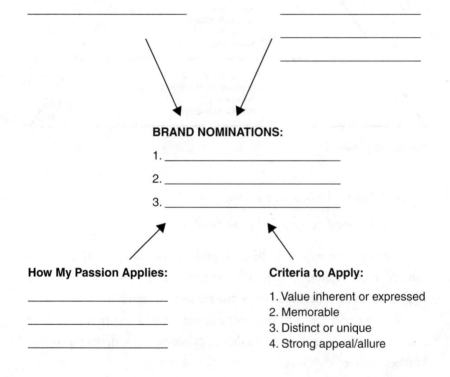

Market Need to Address:

_____

Competencies I Can Apply:

_____

_____

_____

BRAND NOMINATIONS:

1. _____

2. _____

3. _____

How My Passion Applies:

_____

_____

_____

Criteria to Apply:

1. Value inherent or expressed
2. Memorable
3. Distinct or unique
4. Strong appeal/allure

Script

How can I most succinctly capture my competence and its value to the listener so that I'll be remembered, spoken about, and even pursued? What would make me want to contact this person?

FINDING YOUR VALUE PROPOSITION

A value proposition is a brief statement of how people who do business with you improve their condition. It is *not* a mission statement, promotional statement, or brand or core expertise.

Value propositions:

- Offer a compelling reason for the buyer's self-interests to be met.

- Are brief and memorable.

- Can be general or specific.

- Inform the prospect *and remind you* of what is to be gained.

- Are *always* business outcomes, never inputs.

When I was engaged in OD (organizational development) work with Fortune 1000 clients, my value proposition was: *I dramatically improve individual and organizational effectiveness.*

That's it.

I was a generalist, so my value proposition was quite general. If I were more of a specialist, my value proposition could have been: *I reduce the closing time and acquisition costs of new business.*

My advice to those starting out who want quick success is to be generalists. That will increase the number of potential buyers significantly. In my first example, my buyers were anyone who headed a company, major subsidiary, department, division, or any other unit who had budgetary authority for such improvement. In my second example, my buyer would be a vice president or executive director of a sales force.

Generalist versus specialist is the difference between fishing with a huge net or a single rod and reel. You can always throw fish you don't want or can't handle out of the net while you retain the ideal fish. But whatever you get on that rod, you have to pull in one at a time and, even if you win the battle, it could be the wrong fish.

The value proposition keeps *you* focused, as well. You can ask yourself whether a given organization or buyer is appropriate for improving effectiveness at the individual or organizational level (or if sales closing time reduction is right for them).

Value propositions are always *outputs*. Providing workshops or audits or coaching and so forth are all *inputs*. They are deliverables and commodities. They have no intrinsic improvement for the customer of your client. It's the *result* of these inputs that are valuable. Here's an example of the translation:

Input	**Output**
• Strategy retreat	• Increase controlled growth
• Coaching assignment	• Retain top talent more effectively
• Workshop on decision making	• Prioritize best prospects to seek
• Survey customers	• Create higher referral business
• Audit expense procedures	• Reduce nonbusiness expenses
• Evaluate meetings	• Reduce time and duration of meetings

Launch Lesson

Your value proposition gives you the opportunity to begin conversations with a sharp point on the arrow, alerting the other party as to what to focus on in terms of benefit.

Your value proposition can change. I'm not in the consumer (retail) business, marketing to individuals. My current value proposition is: *I create dynamic, global learning communities in which entrepreneurs accelerate the growth of their ventures and themselves.*

Give some thought to what your fundamental improvement in your client's condition will be, reflected in more desirable outputs for the client and client's customers. Another way to ask this is, "After I walk away, how is my client better off?"

Write it here:

_____

_____

The purpose of using this statement as the point of the arrow is to whet someone's appetite, to cause curiosity, to further the conversation, *not to provide answers*. **Never allow your methodology to be your value proposition.** Your methodology is about *how* you do things, not *what* the client receives in terms of an improved condition. Thus, "We provide workshops that enhance sales skills" is never as effective as "We rapidly increase direct sales, repeat business, and referral business." A workshop is a commodity, so I begin to think of prices. But increased sales are results, and so I begin to think of return on the investment if I'm the buyer.

That leads me to the final and most powerful point about value propositions. They generally produce a response such as, "How do you do that?" or "What do you mean?" or "Tell me more." Here is where you take from those very desirable questions:

> *You:* I provide accelerated speed in product commercialization, bringing your products to the right customers rapidly.
>
> *Buyer:* How do you do that?
>
> *You:* Instead of being theoretical, why don't you give me your highest priority product challenges and I'll use those to show you how we'd work together?

Notice what's happened. Instead of launching into a boring, glazed-eyes exegesis about my methodology or technology, I've enabled the buyer to discuss actual, timely, high-value issues that I can use to discuss how important my help would be. This is far better than reciting methodology or providing free consulting. (Always talk about what's needed, but never how it's done. The *what* is marketing, but the *how* is free consulting.)

> **Script**
>
> *We provide dramatic increases in call center personnel abilities to take complaints and turn them into upsell business opportunities. I know that may sound vague, so if you'll tell me your current, worst call center headaches, I'll show you what I'd recommend we do together.*

MOVING FROM AVOCATION TO OCCUPATION

Many of you reading this are entering professional services because you've been providing related types of help to people on an *avocational* basis. That is, you've had an interest, hobby, or pastime that is not only your passion but has helped others.

Now you feel—perhaps very accurately—that you can charge for those services and support yourself doing so. So far, so good; you're in very good company, from Thomas McKinsey to Steve Jobs.

However, you must move *from* being directed by your friends and those who received free help *to* setting your own direction. That means you need a strategy that's purposeful, not random tides and winds.

As you can see from the figure on the next page, you must now direct your business and not allow it to be directed by others.

I helped a consultant in Idaho for free for three years before starting a formal, paying mentor program. Once I did that, he never came back. You can't rely on those gaining free help to direct you because they have very different objectives.

An avocation:

- Can be part-time and fill in available hours
- Requires no marketing, relies on word-of-mouth
- Is often bartering and reciprocal with others

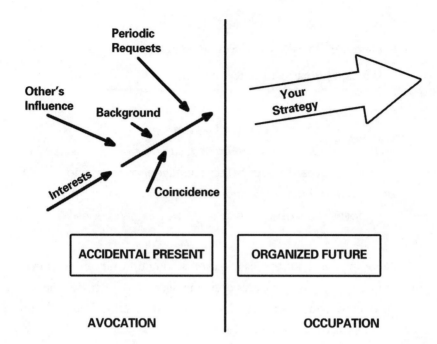

Avocation/Occupation

- Has few, if any, metrics of success
- Is meant primarily to provide freedom for talents
- Is not regulated
- Requires almost no capital investment of upkeep
- Is not competitive

But an occupation:

- Must support living needs
- Requires compliance with rules and regulations
- Is often in highly competitive markets
- Relies on strong promotion
- Requires infrastructure and procedures
- Requires protection of proprietary assets

- Requires ongoing investment in growth
- Has clear indicators of success and failure
- Is meant primarily to generate profit

Launch Lesson

Your conversion from avocation to occupation is unequivocal. You must change your beliefs about your business and demand that you have paying customers, not friends. You are moving from obsession to profession in many cases.

We've spoken about the "easy" part—setting up your office, arranging for insurance, finding sources of financing, and so forth. But the real work is in converting your mental set to a business ethic. You can't run your business as you did your avocation.

Examples of the new you:

- You must be available or responsive during typical business hours.
- You have to invest in marketing, including travel, web presence, collateral, and so on.
- There is no credit or forgiven debts. You charge for your value and demand payment according to your terms.
- You can't be content with your current proficiency, but must constantly build and improve upon it.
- You may want to ally yourself with, or subcontract to, others for help.
- Your presence and renown has to surpass your immediate community.
- You must build *and retain* key client relationships.
- Your value is no longer in your time or presence but rather in your expertise and advice.

Many of you are not caught in this transition, perhaps, but the lesson still pertains. Your prior experience—in a large organization, the military, school, or volunteer work—is no longer a valid reference point for your life as a solo practitioner providing professional services.

You must change your paradigms.

The problem for some of you is that you left your prior position to become independent and free of tyrannical superiors. *You have to ensure that in working for yourself you haven't moved to an even tougher, more unreasonable boss.*

If you understand the new rules and needs, you can adjust your behavior accordingly.

Script

Joan, I'm always flattered that you call me for help, but now this is my business and no longer my hobby. If I helped everyone who asked at no charge, I'd be doing this 100 hours a week and wouldn't be able to feed my family. If you let me know what you need, I'll create a proposal and cite you a fee. But if that doesn't work for you, I understand, and only ask that you understand my position, as well.

IDENTIFYING YOUR SWEET SPOT

If your value statement is an expression you share with clients, educating them about how you improve their condition, your sweet spot is that expertise that is at the core of your business, your fundamental strength.

You don't share this with clients, but use it as your own guide to produce intellectual property and focus on your greatest strengths. One of my coaching clients told me that he had "figured me out": *You have built a business around only doing things* you like and are superbly good at doing.

Remember, if you leave the corporate world to work for yourself, your new boss had better be good to you!

My sweet spot is boutique consulting, meaning that I'm superb at helping solo practitioners and small-firm owners dramatically grow and improve their businesses. Around that sweet spot are spokes that logically emanate from it. Mine would include getting started in consulting, acquiring business, delivering business, and life balance.

You may have three or six spokes, but they should be restricted to those areas most importantly linked to enabling your sweet spot to be utilized. You might call them sub-categories.

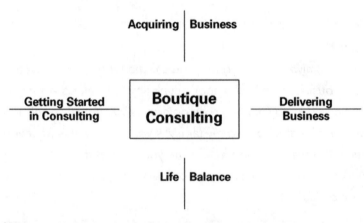

Spokes

The spokes aren't delivery mechanisms (e.g., coaching or design) but rather major issues that enable your sweet spot to be pragmatically utilized.

In the template on the next page, identify your own sweet spot and four key spokes that emanate from it.

The value of this exercise is to force you to organize around just a few high-priority areas. Your intellectual property, conversations, collateral materials, web presence, speaking, and so on, should reinforce and dramatize those spokes. (For example, I've written books entitled

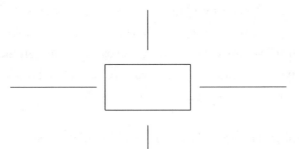

Spokes template

How to Acquire Business, Life Balance, Getting Started in Consulting, and *Process Consulting.* I've also created workshops, podcasts, teleconferences, columns, blog posts, videos, newsletters and so forth around these issues.)

> ### Launch Lesson
> *The way to put a point on your marketing arrow and achieve aerodynamics is to specify for yourself what you're good at and love to do, and promote the heck out of the component parts.*

The spokes may change with time—life balance was a later addition for me—but you should focus on the few that most dramatically convey your sweet spot to practical application among your clients. Here's an example:

> You are: A sales consultant
> Your sweet spot: Decreasing closing time and costs
> Your spokes: Achieving rapid client rapport; providing options; assumptive closes; obtaining referrals.

Your IP*: You create 12 questions that gain the prospect's trust rapidly; you demonstrate how to provide options beyond the usual yes or no: you provide videos and audios on the four types of assumptive close; you create a referral model and software tracking instrument.

IP consists of models, discussions, graphics, delivery mechanisms, ideas, concepts, and similar aids that are uniquely yours and can be provided as marketing and/or delivery tools. IP separates you from the herd. The sweet spot and spokes allow you to organize your IP creation around the most critical areas in which to convey your value to prospects and clients alike.

We're establishing that this is the marketing business. Your value proposition provided to the external world, bolstered by your IP generated by your sweet spot and internal organization, will propel your marketing so that it's easier than ever to be heard above the daily din.

Script

Self-script: What am I superbly good at and passionate about doing that is of value to others, and what are the key components of it that can manifest and convey that value?

BLOWING YOUR OWN HORN

If you don't blow your own horn, there's no music.

One of the most difficult aspects in obtaining business quickly will be the inappropriate sense of humility you probably entertain. Launching and sustaining a new venture is not for the humble. People visit

---

* I'll use this to designate intellectual property from this point on.

churches out of a sense of obligation and the voting booth out of a sense of duty.

Clients are only going to visit you if they believe there is something in it for them—value and an improved condition.

You can't be modest, though you shouldn't be arrogant, either. My definitions:

> **Confidence:** The honest belief that you can help other people.
> **Arrogance:** The honest belief that you have nothing left to learn yourself.
> **Smugness:** Arrogance without the talent.

You have to be supremely confident, and if you occasionally wander over into arrogance, you can always scoot back.

Here are some tips for effective yet harmonious horn-blowing:

- *Adjectives:* Don't merely state that you provide results, or even speedy results. Call them *dramatic.* Other great descriptors: unprecedented, singular, seminal, unheard, renowned, rapid, profound. Advertisers do this all the time. You have to be able to advertise yourself.

- *Evangelists:* Use people who know you and like you (and pretty soon, clients) who will sing your praises. I had a friend who would go to events with a colleague, and they'd each tell people that a very high-powered, exceptional coach was present— and name the other. It was highly effective because they were ostensibly promoting a third party.

- *Trademarks:* We've spoken about protecting your IP with trademarks, service marks, copyright, and registrations. These are visible reminders of a person who is creating unique IP on a regular basis.

- *Web presence:* While SEO (search engine optimization) is useless in selling to corporate buyers, a frequent and even ubiquitous presence in cyberspace is very helpful and provocative. Use your website, blog, articles published on other sites, and similar outlets to raise your profile. Make sure that profile is worth looking at by spending a little (not much at first) on the proper design and photography as required.

- *Outright provocation:* Take contrarian positions. Tackle conventional wisdom. Turn logic upside-down. Stop short of being a performing seal, but do create some discomfort in others' belief systems.

- *Drop names.* Marshall Goldsmith, the übercoach, was asked at one of my Thought Leadership Conferences how best to become a thought leader. He said, "Hang out with them." (He literally carried Peter Drucker's briefcase.) Network and chat with them at events. Then say, "I was talking to Alan Weiss and Malcolm Gladwell the other day at an event, and the three of us agree . . ." (See, I just did it!)

It's best if your horn is augmented, so try to build a support system that will sustain the sound. You *don't* want to be with people who keep telling you that you have to have more humility. You want to be with people who keep telling you, "Stop holding back: sing your praises!"

Launch Lesson

The first sale is to yourself. If you can't become impassioned and excited about how you can help others, and generate a contagious enthusiasm, then perhaps you should go into woodworking or philately, where loud noises are unwelcome and you generally work alone.

Write down five strengths you have that can absolutely, dramatically help other people, and then write how they would help. I've provided one example:

Strength	**Help**
Good writer	Critique and edit materials rapidly

1. _____   _____

2. _____   _____

3. _____   _____

4. _____   _____

5. _____   _____

Practice talking about these relationships in strong, compelling terms. For example: "I can review, critique, and rewrite your promotional material in 24 hours so that your initiatives proceed rapidly but with the added benefit of incredibly persuasive language and irresistible offers."

It's not hard, but you do have to overcome the false modesty bit. We are inculcated from young ages to show humility, not to lord it over others, to beware of arrogance, and to "fit in." However, none of those people (or you) were aware you would one day try to be a huge success in the marketing business, which, at times, calls for precisely that type of behavior.

I know what you're thinking: "I know humble people who do quite well." Maybe so. But I'll tell you my unequivocal findings from 30 years in the marketing business: The best salespeople you'll ever encounter *believe in their heart of hearts that they are the best salespeople anywhere, and they'll tell you that.* The same applies to doctors, firefighters, reporters, nurses, athletes, performers, CEOs—anyone who is really passionate about their profession and their work *believes* they are the best *and is unafraid to demonstrate it.*

You need to tell people how good you are because you want to create the gravity to attract them to you, thereby mitigating the need to provide tons of credibility and erasing any pressure on fees, both of which are urgent positions for anyone wanting to secure business in their first 90 days.

> **Script**
>
> *I provide strategic guidance and commitment so that every employee acts as an owner of the business and makes the right decisions every day to create dramatic growth and tighten cost control.*

MILLION DOLLAR CONSULTING® MARKET GRAVITY

The more quickly you can establish some gravity to draw prospective buyers to you, the more quickly you'll gain business *without the need to establish credibility or haggle over fees.* That's because when people come to you, they intend to do business.

No one walks into McDonald's to browse.

> **Launch Lesson**
>
> *Cold calling and direct mail are for selling lawn care and high-interest loans. When you knock on doors, you have to prove that you're good to cynical buyers, but when people knock on your door, you merely have to see if you can fit them into your calendar.*

As you can see on the facing page, there is a wealth of alternative routes to use to draw people to you. I have used or continue to use all of them. However, we're talking about the first 90 days of a new launch, so I want to address your attention to the most propitious for

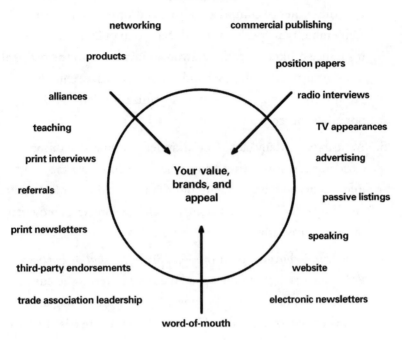

pro bono work

networking   commercial publishing

products

position papers

alliances   radio interviews

teaching   TV appearances

print interviews   advertising

Your value, brands, and appeal

referrals   passive listings

print newsletters   speaking

third-party endorsements   website

trade association leadership   electronic newsletters

word-of-mouth

Market gravity

quick business. (But by all means, attempt as many as you're comfortable engaging in—you cannot do too much marketing.)

1. *Referrals:* We talked earlier and provided a script for contacting everyone you know. Make a list, set priorities, call the highest priorities, and confidently ask for referrals. This is included under gravity because your contacts will be drawing people to you. *The first issues to deal with when you get names:*

   - Ascertain that the person is truly a buyer, someone who can write a check*.
   - Seek only to set up a personal appointment, never try to sell anything over the phone.

---

* Authorizing a check is as good as writing one these days.

2. *Speaking:* Speak anywhere you can on your expertise, provided that the audience comprises buyers and/or recommenders. Remember that speaking for a local group of 20 in an insurance brokerage could get you an invitation to the regional or even corporate office. Chambers of commerce, church groups, civic groups, and service organizations are excellent potential sources.

3. *Networking:* Many clubs (social, athletic, business) sponsor enrichment sessions after hours where someone speaks informally about investments, or business practices, or real estate, and similar topics. If you belong to a club, volunteer to present a session, arrive early, and stay afterward.

4. *Publishing:* Forget about the *Wall Street Journal* or *Fortune*. Write an article, column, op-ed piece, or letter to the editor in your local daily or weekly newspaper, business magazine, monthly magazine, and so forth. Make your expertise known, especially about local topics that people are ardently following. (See the appendix for an example of an inquiry letter to an editor.)

5. *Breakfast meetings:* Invite 50–60 potential buyers (at relatively similar levels) to a breakfast on an irresistible topic (e.g., "How to choose and retain top talent inexpensively," or "How to maximize customer referral business"). You'll get about 12–15 attendees if you're persistent. Buy a buffet breakfast in a private room of a top hotel or club, and spend the hour in a brief presentation, facilitation of discussion, and summary of learning points. Then send a summary to the 45 people who didn't come and offer to meet with them privately.

These are some of the aggressive gravity techniques you should consider undertaking very quickly. They are the few ways I know that reliably can produce short-term business. Moreover, as you engage in them, word-of-mouth and viral marketing will spread, especially if you initiate three or four concurrently. These are far superior to knocking on doors and calling strangers.

> **Script**
> *Please join me for a highly valuable discussion of the critical issue of retaining top customers. You'll be with a dozen owners (executives) like yourself and you'll be back at your desk in time to start your normal day, but armed with vital new techniques to immediately solidify your key business base. Breakfast will be provided. Limited seating.*

SUMMARY OF THE FIRST 30 DAYS

Prior to your launch if you have the time, or in the first week, if the transition was unexpected, you should have created a contact list of everyone you know in every capacity, examined and made plans for normal and contingency financing, determined where you will work physically, and created a support network.

Ideally, all that was done before Day One, but, in any case, done in the very first few days.

You should secure legal and accounting help, acquire basic equipment and supply needs, and begin scheduling the next two to three weeks or more. Be aware that it's as important to *ignore* irrelevant advice (no matter how well intentioned) as it is to find good advice and listen to it.

By the second week, you should be creating a brand (or even brands), solidifying your value proposition, identifying your sweet spot and consequent key components, and begin broadcasting what you're doing.

By the fourth week, you should have engaged in or fully planned speeches wherever you can find buyers and recommenders, set up breakfasts or enrichment sessions, called everyone on that list you created for referrals and meetings, sent out publishing inquiries, set up an elementary website, and begun networking at least twice a week.

That's the initial month. You might well have moved to a proposal or even business if you've been aggressive and had the benefit of advance planning.

Thirty days is plenty of time to accomplish what I've outlined above in a methodical, disciplined manner. But it won't work if you're sitting by the phone, waiting for it to ring.

PART I REVIEW

It's one thing to read about what you should do, but it's another to actually *do it!*

BEHAVIORAL AND ENVIRONMENTAL FACTORS

I'm continually sensitive to that fact as I coach people globally and want to tackle it here. You may be reading this book straight through, intending to go back and attack the individual suggestions, or you may be trying to implement what you learn along the way. In either case, we should bear in mind small business guru David Maister's classic line: "We know what to do, but we still don't do it!"

The first 30 days of your new practice might not mean ultimate success or failure, but it can establish good and bad habits without your even realizing it. Remember that you only get one first impression. A single key referral source who is approached poorly because of a lack of planning and preparation will have long-term deleterious effects. Conversely, a key contact from your prior company who is correctly nurtured might mean a rapid contract.

Here are some of the behavioral and environmental factors that can subliminally influence you, and some techniques to avoid being subverted and focus on rapid success.

1. The good intentioned but nonknowing

These are people who sincerely care for you, even love you, and want to offer every kind of support and assistance. The problem is that they are uneducated about your type of professional services work.

61

Consequently, they will advise you to try things that work elsewhere ("Just pick up the phone and call people") or that are common myths ("Divide what you need to live on by available working hours, and there's your daily fee"). Since the advice comes with the best intentions, it's often tough to ignore or reject.

You should be grateful to all those who want to help you. Accept the advice as given, but *do not implement it* unless and until you're convinced it will apply and improve your success rate. Your prospective clients aren't listening to everyone who gives them ideas; hence, you have to make a pragmatic case for the use of your help. The same applies to family and friends trying to help you. Be gracious but not gullible.

2. The projectionists

There are people who have tried what you are attempting, with varying levels of success. Some will tend to project on to you their own successes and failures. They may tell you to eschew networking because they've had no success with it, and to pursue direct mail because they've had some success with it.

Projectionists fear that if you're immediately good at something they are not good at (or weren't immediately) that somehow they are inferior to your talents. So they'll assume—consciously or unconsciously—that you are their equal (or slightly inferior). Their advice will be rooted in that belief.

Don't listen to just anyone who tells you what works and what doesn't. *Even those with demonstrable success* may be giving you advice that truly worked for them but can't possibly work for you. They may have had college contacts, or clients whose family they know, or just great luck. If you read most executive biographies, from Lee Iacocca to Steve Jobs, you'll find they are fascinating, but not people whom you can emulate. They were successful in singular conditions with unique backgrounds and situational timing.

Cull your advice using the criteria in this books and a realistic assessment of your own particular behaviors, passions, education, experience, and background.

3. The investors

Some of you will have taken loans or arranged credit. Those investors, whether family, banks, or friends, may feel they have the right to advise you on your plans.

When you accept money, make it clear that you're not offering some kind of advisory position in return. Keep the transaction formal: a written agreement with repayment terms over a certain period. Never offer ownership in your endeavor.

I've found that bankers, attorneys, accountants, and others really don't understand others' businesses except through their own filters (e.g., cash flow, protection, taxes), and are overwhelmingly conservative to begin with, and more so when they have money at stake. It's impossible to grow rapidly and strongly when you're conservative and risk averse.

Moreover, family investors don't even have to say anything other than, "How's business?" at a dinner table or event to begin to cause discomfort. Your reply should be "Fine." and you should meet your repayment schedule religiously.

Better yet: Try not to accept family money or contributions from friends. I recommend that to the extreme of *not* doing business with family or friends. Most who have find they ruin the friendship and/or their business.

4. Premature panic

Weeks can go by with nothing happening other than your own continuing efforts. That is, you won't receive a return call, there will be no mail, you'll feel your ideas have dried up, and it will seem your boat is becalmed.

That's why the title of this book isn't *The First Nine Hours* or *The First Nine Days*. Business winds are variable in the extreme. The key is not to panic.

Use the subheadings in the first three chapters of this book to plot out high-potential activities: consolidate your contacts and call; create your brand or brands; identify your sweet spot; begin creating market gravity routes. You need to be active every day, with a sense of both accomplishment and progress. If you panic at this early stage, you'll actually undermine these tasks even if you do them, sort of like a singer whose voice is off key or an artist whose hands shake.

Stay with your regimen and don't allow yourself to think that "It's not working!" this early in the game.

5. The sense of overwhelm

My intent is to keep you busy and focused over the first 30 days. That should help you direct your energy and thinking to those most important activities and away from the peripheral and wrong directions.

You can't do everything at once. Plan your day with a physical calendar (electronic calendars don't permit you to see a week or month at a time). Try to get three priorities accomplished every day, then spend some time with the less important (e.g., definitely make three calls for referrals, and if you have the time rearrange your work space for more comfort).

The best way to avoid feeling overwhelmed—and it's a feeling, not a fact, by the way—is to *control* your life by scheduling what has to be done on a limited-priority basis. This will give you the accomplishment and progress you need to be in control. Don't wake up in the morning wondering what you should do that day or thinking you can play it by ear. The most important thing, perhaps, about the first 30 days is not to waste them through poor planning and lack of discipline.

PRIVATE TIME AND PUBLIC TIME

You'll find an interesting challenge in deciding how to spend your time, which can be utilized like a well-tuned engine or dissipated like a broken-down jalopy.

There is a thin but important line between gathering support and wasting your time. You should try to spend time at associations, meetings, and events that can boost your progress and build your base. You should avoid spending time with people like yourself who may merely be intent on commiserating about poor progress or lying about how well they're doing.

Service clubs such as Rotary and community groups such as soccer leagues or environmental campaigns should be investigated to ascertain whether the members can serve as prospects, referral sources, and/or sounding boards. There's nothing wrong with supporting great causes, of course, but there *is* something wrong with expecting your mere involvement to generate business for you.

Professional groups—realty, design, consulting, coaching, accounting, and so forth—may be the source of new ideas and reciprocal help, or they may merely be a place where others gather to pretend they're actually building their businesses and perfecting their crafts. One or two meetings as a guest should make that evident. Some key considerations:

- Are they focused on better marketing?
- Do they provide help, tutorials, mentoring, and examples?
- Are there unequivocally successful people attending?
- Are they known and respected among prospects and members of the greater community?

If you join mastermind groups, make sure that you're not the smartest person in the room or on the call. These expert groups should last no more than six months and provide access to others who:

1. You can learn from.
2. Are willing to share.

Above all, stay away from groups and individuals who merely seek to sell you products or services. You shouldn't be spending money on these items, and they're usually sold by people who *solely* sell to those trying to build a practice, since they've never been able to sell to the buyers you, yourself, are seeking.

There are more people trying to coach professional services providers than there are successful professional services providers.

THE RISKS OF HUMILITY

We are inculcated from a very young age to be humble. This originates from early schooling and the need to coexist with other students; from the politically correct self-esteem emphasis (one school in Oregon gave out 20 valedictorian awards, especially ludicrous); from religious and spiritual admonishment about not being vainglorious; and from parents who often were able to succeed by not offending anyone and staying off the radar.

It's fine to be humble in terms of our place in the universe and having respect for others and our environment. But we seriously retard our progress when we are humble about our own capacity to contribute and help others.

Picasso is rumored to have said that his mother told him if he went into the clergy he'd become Pope; that if he entered the military he'd become a great general; and that if he became a merchant, he'd become a wealthy man. "But," he said, "I chose to paint and became Picasso."

Great successes do not have small egos, because a strong ego is required to accept rejection, to overcome objection, and to take prudent (and sometimes greater) risk. You needn't brag or boast, but being reticent and humble will not help acquire business. The very buyers you are courting are usually powerful, successful people who prefer to deal with powerful, successful people.

Our motto, repeated in this book, is "If you don't blow your own horn, there's no music." If you're not confident enough to express your talents boldly and clearly, why would anyone else? You don't want to develop advocates who merely represent you; you want to create evangelists who will convert others to believe in you.

No matter what your former job or position—and especially if you were fired, downsized, or otherwise involuntarily removed—*do not let that experience create a sense of inferiority.* Many of us—including myself—only succeed after we were fired. More Fortune 500 companies were created during the Great Depression than at any other time.

Buyers appreciate confidence, not diffidence.

THE REAL APPEAL OF MARKETING GRAVITY

This is a term I coined in the mid-nineties. It refers to the ability to attract people to you. Since there are only two types of buyer contact—reaching out or being approached—I realized that there were significant differences and these were not coequal options.

When you reach out, you must prove yourself. You are intruding on someone else. The range is shown below:

Cold call … Direct mail … Meeting at an event … Referral … Approach

With a cold call or direct mail, you are asking someone totally unfamiliar with you to hear your appeal. When you meet at an event—for example, by networking—you have made contact on the spot. With a referral, you are at least able to use a third party who knows you.

With all of those devices, ranging from cold to lukewarm, you must answer these explicit or implicit questions:

What can I do for you?
What can you do for me?
Why should I invest time with you?
Are you different from every other seller?
Can I delegate you to someone else?

You can see that these filters are severe and hard to overcome.

However, when someone approaches you, their questions are quite different:

> How can we work together?
> Can you do for me what you've done for others?
> How can I learn more about your work?
> Will you be interested in working with me?

You can see that the dynamic is quite different. Not only is there no credibility issue, *but fees are seldom an issue when someone approaches you.*

Hence, I saw that while two approaches existed, only one made sense for solo practitioners and boutique firms. Then I realized that this gravity can take place well within 90 days, so why wait to create it? You don't need, counterintuitively, a huge body of work or long client list.

Here are the best, early routes for you on my gravity wheel.

1. Speak wherever possible: Speak for free to hone your skills (Toastmasters and local service clubs are good for that), but then speak wherever you can find buyers and recommenders. Try the Chamber of Commerce, local chapters of national organizations (American Institute of Architects, Florida Bankers Association, large local offices of major realty or insurance firms).

2. Publish provocatively in the media: Write op-eds (opposite the editorial page) for local newspapers. Write letters to the editor. Submit columns to local business publications and request a column.*

3. Have third parties mention and endorse you: These are referrals that pursue you instead of you pursuing them. Have your dentist, lawyer, accountant, designer, landscaper, and so forth think of people to send to you who can profit from your value proposition. If you belong to a club, offer to be part of an enrichment series in which you present your ideas to members.

4. Create a splash on the web: Use a blog (newsletters require a subscription base; blogs do not) to trumpet (blow your horn) your ideas in your area of expertise. But make them bold and contrarian. Draw attention to issues by looking at them in new ways. I began my very early publicity, before there was the advantage of the Internet, by proclaiming that quality efforts usually didn't work and were a waste of time.

You will always be better served when people come to you. So there's one final dynamic to marketing gravity that I want to emphasize that doesn't appear obviously on the chart.

You need to become an OOI: Object of Interest. You can't be the 450,000th person talking about leaders having to walk their talk. You

---

* Two good sources: *National Trade and Professional Organizations of the U.S.* (Columbia Books; hard copy, online, and in libraries) and *Writer's Market*, published by Writer's Digest.

have to be the first person talking about them having to talk their walk. (For example: Leaders should be examples, but also have to publicize and openly communicate how things are to be done.) In these professions, you can't be loathe to stand out in a crowd, and you can't worry about being liked.

One of the huge downsides of being involved in some of those professional associations I referenced—where everyone simply strives for internal recognition—is that there is tremendous pressure to conform, to support, and to be mainstream. Believe me, that is not how you start and grow a professional practice, unless you want to be swamped in the mainstream.

Be bold enough to be different.

THE SECOND 30 DAYS

CLOSE ENCOUNTERS
OF THE CLIENT KIND

We're about one month into your new venture and it's time to bring the first piece of business on board if you haven't done so yet. That's right: This month at the latest you receive your first check, wire, credit card, or old jewelry in compensation for your value.

You will be approximately 6–12 months ahead of most people starting their own professional services practice.

FINDING THAT ELUSIVE AND IMPORTANT NUMBER ONE

Let's start with the acquisition, and we'll talk about broader practices later in this chapter. Bringing on board that all-important first client sometimes means reasonable compromises and learning that people will pay for value.

If you left your former employer with a positive relationship and the promise or hint of external consulting work, now is the time to collect your chips. Contact the person who can authorize your help, and set up a meeting.

Launch Lesson

E-mail is one dimensional, phone is two dimensional, and personal contact three dimensional. Why be a cardboard figure when you can be an interactive and dynamic influence?

Script

I'd like to pursue our earlier discussion of my help on a consulting basis. What's the best date and time for you?

Never try to hold this meeting by phone. You may feel safer that way, but you'll wind up poorer. It's harder to say no eye to eye and in proximity. If you feel awkward on the phone (to make appointments) or in person, practice with a partner. If you feel you just can't do it, stop reading at this point and look for a job in an auto dealership where prospects come to you.

If you have no such relationship with a prior employer, then use the call-everyone-you-know list and choose those people who were most receptive and helpful. Call six of them and say, "I'm moving on the next phase and would like to pursue some work with you or with someone you would be willing to introduce me to." The very worst thing they can say is no. No one is shooting at you.

If you have no such warm prospects on your list—which is rare and leads me to believe you weren't very disciplined or thorough with your list—then go to a nonprofit and volunteer your services for a short-term project. Don't tell them you're new in the business; tell them you contribute to the community every year, and you're pursuing such contribution with them. Find a nonprofit that:

- Is a cause you truly believe in.
- Will use you in a public way, not at home, calling people for donations.

- Has a high-visibility board of high potential to you.
- Will be willing to provide testimonials and referrals.

Pursue the executive director for your offer of pro bono work. It's ideal to work at the senior levels with top management, the board, key donors, and so on. This should be your springboard to a completed project, reference, testimonial, contacts, and referrals. You can see the huge return on your investment here.

Through one or more of these actions, follow this sequence. It may take you one meeting or three, a week or a month. If it goes beyond three meetings and/or a month, you should move on to your next prospect.

1. Identify the true buyer, the person who can authorize payment for your value and who has objectives you can meet. *Do NOT settle for lower-level nonbuyers.* You'll waste your time even if they're willing to meet with you.

2. Enter into a conversation (not a pitch) to ascertain the outcomes (objectives) they would like to achieve, how they would know there was improvement (metrics), and what the impact of success would be (value).

3. Create a proposal with three options of increasing value to meet those objectives with increasing value and increasing fees. (See the appendix for a proposal example.)

4. Set a date, time, and action to discuss that proposal (e.g., Friday at 10 a.m. on the phone—in person is not necessary). Get the proposal to the buyer within 24–48 hours electronically and/or by FedEx.

5. Follow up as planned and ask, "Which option makes the most sense for us to pursue?"

I know this sounds somewhat simple. It is. It's not *easy*, but it is simple. (Don't forget, our job is to make the complex simple.)

If you pursue 15 sources, get meetings with 10, get permission to present a proposal to 5, *you should close one piece of business*. If it's the pro bono work, look at it as a huge leverage to gain three or four pieces of business from the contacts and referrals. You can do this in your second month of business. I'll pursue the details in the following segments.

Just bear in mind:

- Be disciplined and schedule your work and plans.
- Be fearless in calling people and asking for meetings.
- Be clear on your value proposition.
- Express confidence and enthusiasm that you can help.
- Press for a next action, date, and time *always*.

Script

Linda, I recall that you were friendly with Tom at Acme Widgets, and from my earlier discussion with you, I have some ideas on how I can help him and Acme in my new role. Would you be willing to either introduce me directly or allow me to use your name in contacting him?

MARKETING FOR FREE

Some of you may have some money to invest at this point, but I'm working on the assumption that money is tight and what you can do for free is always an advantage. Since I've noted that this *is* the marketing business, how can you best do that without spending a bundle?

What you need more than anything at this point is visibility. You need to separate yourself from the herd and create a high-rise profile on the plateau of service providers all around you. Here are my suggestions for doing this:

- Perform pro bono work. Find an arts group or charity with significant clout and propose a project over the short term.

Case Study

I was on the board of a shelter for battered women and offered to lead them in strategy formulation over the course of several meetings. One of the board members was the local chief of police. He asked if I could do the same work for the police department, and just as I was about to tell him that I couldn't do more work for free, he said the magic words: "I have a government grant."

- If you belong to a club (social, athletic, service), offer an enrichment night in which you provide a facilitated session about your expertise and it's worth to anyone interested for 90 minutes in the evening. Many clubs have such features in place as a matter of routine. You may be able to do it somewhere even though you're not a member.

- Speak at local groups such as Rotary, chambers of commerce, and church groups. This will hone your skills, as well as serve as a potential referral source. Most of these types of groups have luncheon or evening speakers.

- Find local chapters of trade and professional organizations and volunteer to speak. This could be the local chapter of the American Institute of Architects, state Realtors association, or accounting professional association. (If you want to hone your skills, try Toastmasters, which is a good resource to practice your speaking in a safe and low-threat environment.)

Launch Lesson

Approach the executive director or equivalent in these initiatives. If they can't use you immediately, ask for a good time to follow up. And offer to be a replacement should a scheduled speaker not be able to make it.

- Assume highly controversial or provocative approaches. This will depend on your boldness and risk tolerance, but you'll stand out far more readily if you tell people that you have to educate the buyer to buy rather than the seller to sell, for example. You don't stand out on the plateau by sticking with the herd. Do this in your blogging, newsletters, and articles.

- Write letters to the editor of newspapers and magazines when they've published material that bears on your expertise and gives you an excuse to agree or disagree as an expert. (Yes, agreeing is fine.) Consider submitting an op-ed piece to the local newspaper. There's usually an editorial page editor to whom you can write with your inquiry for the article.

- Don't be bashful. I can't tell you how many people have told me that their uncle or father-in-law or cousin knows important potential buyers, but they're afraid to be impositions. If you have value to share, then you're creating a win/win/win, not an imposition. Ask. They may say no, but you won't be harmed. And they may just be overjoyed to help.

Case Study

A woman new to consulting told me that she and her neighbor alternated barbecues every Sunday. She didn't know the neighbor's husband too well but did know he was an executive vice president at the largest bank downtown.

"I can't ask to see him while I serve him a hot dog," she said.

"Tell him you'd like to stop by because you have some banking best practices you want to run by him, and don't let go of your end of the hot dog until he says 'yes,'" I told her.

She got the appointment and a project.

- Seek out local consultants and boutique firms and offer to do subcontract work. You'll learn how they market, learn how to deliver, make some money, and substantially increase your visibility.

- Offer value on social media platforms. These are not high-potential sources because they're their own plateau with everyone diligently self-promoting. But if you offer value every day instead of simply extolling yourself or asking for "likes," you may just draw some attention.

Case Study

At this writing, I have about 6,000 followers on Twitter, and I follow no one. Every day I place three postings of value, not unlike the advice in this book. It takes less than two minutes.

I draw attention—and wrath—because I have all those followers but follow no one. And attention is what you need.

Before you spend money marketing, try doing it on the cheap. You'll be more successful than you would have imagined.

Script

My expertise is in financial planning, especially in turbulent times. I thought your members [give the demographics of the club] might appreciate the opportunity to hear about this and ask some questions. I will not sell a thing and will not be self-promotional. I thought this might be a timely and important benefit for your members.

CREATING PIPELINES

In marketing, a pipeline is a conductor of leads and potential business to you. Like an oil or water pipeline, the marketing pipeline can get clogged, spring leaks, need cleaning, and collect unwanted sediment.

The best pipelines allow a strong flow of the desired resources, as shown below.

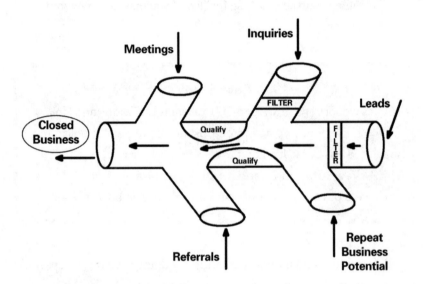

The marketing pipeline

Ideally, leads enter your pipeline only after they are qualified. But you should have filters in the pipes so that inappropriate leads are kept out of the main flow. (These are organizations that are the wrong size, or not appropriate for your expertise, or the lead is at a level too low to move forward.)

Note above that some leads enter a long way off and will need considerable time to reach the end of the pipe. Others enter along the way, and some in a manner that present opportunity almost immediately.

Ideally, your business should have leads flowing at a variety of distances, so that the pipes are full of appropriate flow.

There are basically four sources of leads:

1. Those that you unearth yourself in the marketing methods we've spoken about to this point.

2. Those that come to you via a referral from others.

3. Those that come to you from existing business that expands and/or renews.

4. Those who find you by design or accident: on your website, blog, newsletter, random meetings, and so on.

> ### Launch Lesson
> *You have to maintain your pipeline, even when you're engaged on a project. If the pipeline is empty, it is extremely hard to rapidly refill it, and you'll lose momentum.*

In Steven Spielberg's great movie *Close Encounters of the Third Kind*, it is stipulated that the first kind is a sighting (of aliens or their craft); the second is physical evidence found; and the third is actual contact. You need to go through the same sequence: Sight your prospects, get evidence of them, and meet them.

Leads are the lifeblood of your business. They come from different directions, are at varying stages of interaction and familiarity, and move at different speeds. You can't have too many of them.

That means you can never cease collecting names. You don't do business with organizations but rather with people in those organizations. And you meet all types of other people along the way. Add them to your FileMaker Pro or in an Excel file.

Some names can become true leads or provide you with leads. Some leads may not turn out to flow through the pipeline, but they may be valuable enough to retain for other reasons. To avoid clogging up your pipeline with nonleads, put the names in separate categories. A true lead is someone who is capable of doing business with you and is in some stage of interest, whether holding an appointment or actively reviewing a proposal.

They are called leads for a reason. They start something.

Script

Self-script: Is this someone who I believe is capable of authorizing a project and approving payment for the kind of value I provide? Where are they in that sequence, and how do I best move them forward?

CREATING AND QUALIFYING LEADS

One of the fundamental methods to fill your pipeline with *quality* leads is to assess what you find and what comes to you. By quality leads, I mean:

- A true economic buyer (someone who can authorize a check)
- Someone who is appropriate for your particular value
- Someone who has a realistic need you can fill

You have limited time and energy. Not every lead is a good lead, just as not all business is good business. As you determine whom to pursue, and evaluate those who approach you, there has to be some objective method to assess potential and the investment you will make. Call it an ROL, or return on leads.

One of the main reasons service providers feel overwhelmed and miss priorities and deadlines is that they chase everything, like a dog that keeps looking for squirrels it will never catch, while a rabbit is hiding under a bush a few feet away. Everything you see can't be allowed to distract you.

Consequently, your ideal prospects will have ideal traits that you configure and your actual prospects can be compared against that ideal, no less than a wine receives a score relative to 100. You know anything above 90 is probably a safe choice and worth the investment.

I've developed a scoring system to help you in the critical initial 90 days to spend your prospecting time wisely and fill your pipeline with a strong flow and no clogs.

THE MILLION DOLLAR CONSULTING® QUALIFYING SYSTEM TEMPLATE

Substitute your own criteria and ratings as appropriate. I've filled in the content to illustrate the usage. It's a great idea to run every prospective client through this quickly. (Just because you only have a few leads doesn't mean you should pursue them if they're not potentially valuable. You'd be better off spending the time on further marketing.)

Instructions:

1. List your ideal traits for a potential client.
2. Rate those traits based on 10 as highest and 1 as lowest. You may have more than one 10 or any other number.
3. Fill in the actual traits that your prospect possesses.
4. Score your prospect's actual traits against each ideal, with a 10 being a perfect fit and a 0 being a total mismatch.
5. Multiply the rating times the score in each category.
6. Add up the rated scores to get a total.
7. Compare the total against the ideal total (all 10s in scoring) and come up with a percentage of the ideal.
8. Decide which percentage minimum is required for follow-up and with what priority and apply. I recommend nothing below 80 percent.

Note: If you don't have enough information to complete your own form, then do some further homework. It will be worth it.

Qualifying System and Template

Ideal Traits	Rating
• History of using consultants	7
• Within a day trip of my home	2
• Services or financial industries	6
• Minimum of 250 employees	8
• Financially strong/stable	9
• Buyer easily identifiable	10

Ideal Traits	Rating	Actual
• History of using consultants	7	Use constantly
• Within a day trip of my home	2	Overnight trip
• Services or financial industries	6	Mortgage lending
• Minimum of 250 employees	8	625 people
• Financially strong/stable	9	#3 in the industry
• Buyer easily identifiable	10	VP operations

Ideal Traits	Rating	Actual	Score
• History of using consultants	7	Use constantly	10
• Within a day trip of my home	2	Overnight trip	0
• Services or financial industries	6	Mortgage lending	10
• Minimum of 250 employees	8	625 people	7
• Financially strong/stable	9	#3 in the industry	8
• Buyer easily identifiable	10	VP operations	8

Ideal Traits	Rating	Actual	Score	R × S
● History of using consultants	7	Use constantly	10	70
● Within a day trip of my home	2	Overnight trip	0	0
● Services or financial industries	6	Mortgage lending	10	60
● Minimum of 250 employees	8	625 people	7	56
● Financially strong/stable	9	#3 in the industry	8	72
● Buyer easily identifiable	10	VP operation	8	80
		Total Rated Score:		338
		Total Possible Score:		420
		TRS %:		80%

In my example, the maximum R/S possible (all scores of 10 in every category) would be 420. The actual candidate scored 338, which is 80 percent, or a low B.

Once you have created your template, you can use it fairly quickly each time. You'll find out if you need to do more homework to fill in key criteria.

> **Launch Lesson**
>
> *Worse than chasing squirrels is chasing your own tail. Don't get spun around by every person who exhibits interest or asks for information. Leads are qualitative not quantitative when you are a solo practitioner.*

When you create and qualify leads—you pursue them or they come to you—never ignore ROL. You're better off with three carefully vetted prospects than two dozen worthless ones. Don't let your ego get in the way. The salesperson in a Bentley dealership knows that most people making even detailed inquiries about a car will never buy one. The salesperson needs to use judgment and careful questioning to determine which deserve investment and pursuit.

> ### Script
>
> *Is this lead with an economic buyer who can use my value and who has a history of acquiring outside help, or can this person quickly lead me to that buyer?*

GETTING PAID

Too many people prepare for failure and not success, so they're ready to atone and compensate, but not exploit and capitalize. I have more faith and so should you.

You may be getting your first business at about this time. It may be for $1,000 or $25,000 or more, but it's early and well done. However, the point isn't merely doing business; it's about receiving equitable compensation for your value. And it's never what you make that's important, it's what you *keep*.

That's called a margin, and represents the money left for you from an engagement after all relevant expenses have been paid. Since your travel and lodging expenses are typically paid by the client, and your fixed expenses are small working out of your home or shared office, margins in this business should be significant. I typically keep about 90 percent of what I bill, which is a margin all corporations would kill for.

Ideally, you should be paid on commencement of a project for any small assignment, e.g., a day of coaching, a workshop, design samples, financial reviews, and so on. For longer and more complex assignments, you may have payment terms, such as:

- 50 percent due on commencement
- 50 percent due 45 days from commencement

> ### Launch Lessons
> *Always establish payment terms of maximum benefit to you. Never negotiate fees, but you can negotiate terms, so start with the best possible condition, just in case. Sometimes the buyer will simply say, "Fine."*

Here is a hierarchy of favorable payment terms, from best to worst:

1. Payment in advance upon signing. To stimulate this, offer a small discount (5 to 10 percent) for full payment in this manner. *Some organizations have rules that any such discount* must *be accepted, and you'll trigger the payment.*

> ### Case Study
> For several years, my top buyer at my top client, pharmaceutical manufacturer Merck, retained my services for $250,000 a year and paid me on January 2, taking a 10 percent ($25,000) discount.
>
> One year, I asked him if 10 percent was the right amount as a rule, or if 5 percent would have been as attractive, to get some advice for other prospects. He shocked me when he said, "I don't care about the amount of the discount, I pay you so that the company can't cancel my project should any downturns or other priorities arise."
>
> Moral: Position the advance payment in the *buyer's* self-interest, not your own.

2. 50 percent at commencement and 50 percent in 45 days (always use relative days, not calendar days, because things can be delayed or change).

3. A percentage at commencement and lesser or equal percentages during the project, e.g., 30-30-25-15.

Never—never—agree to be paid at the conclusion of the project or intervention. You'll find the project will never end. There will always be something else (scope seep) because the missing payments are leverage. Conversely, when you're paid in full prior to the end of the project, *you* have the leverage of stopping work if the client doesn't meet commitments and deadlines, or becomes abusive.

Similarly, do not accept "performance" participation, sometimes called "contingency fees." This means you share in a portion of the results of the project or firm's growth. For every instance of a Microsoft secretary who took stock and was eventually worth $20 million, there are 20 million examples of professionals who never received a penny for their value and hard work from such offers (typically suggested by start-up operations).

As a start-up yourself, you can't afford noncash offers. The same applies for bartering services.* Always demand and accept only cash. Make sure that you can accept wire transfers (some companies prefer them) and credit cards (some government agencies and small businesses prefer them). You can set up a merchant account for credit cards (MasterCard, Visa, Discover) with the bank with which you do business and, separately, with American Express.

When you are not paid on time, whether for your fee or expense reimbursement (sample invoices appear in the appendix), never argue with lower-level people—accounts payable, purchasing, and so forth. Go back to your buyer. Explain that there is an issue with payment and you would appreciate him or her stepping in. Your buyer can either expedite the late payment or authorize a manual check outside the system. ("Payment in 30 days" merely means the invoice sits on someone's desk for 29 days.)

---

* Bartered services are fully taxable by the IRS in the United States, and must be reported on income tax forms. You could lose your shirt with these offers.

Your final leverage is to stop work and keep what you have been paid (hence, the payments toward the front end), though it will seldom come to that. As a rule, never start work until your initial payment has been received. The major problems are with smaller companies guarding cash flow and some larger firms with huge bureaucracies.

Script

With your buyer: We have a problem. I'm meeting our contractual agreement for implementation, but your payment people are not meeting the contractual agreement for my fee (reimbursements). Would you contact them and let me know later today when I can expect the overdue payment? I'm sure you must have similar issues with your own customers. Thanks for your help.

Cash is king. Pursue the royal road.

5

CREATING YOUR DIGITAL EMPIRE

My friend and the technical strategist behind all of my cyberspace presence, Chad Barr, coined the term *digital empire.** I interpret this as the realm you create, inhabit, and rule on the web.

The boundaries of that empire are seldom fixed, but there are dead ends and black holes, as well as exploding stars and uncontrolled asteroids. In this chapter we'll talk about the vast Internet *in terms of strategic and tactical marketing, not in terms of technology.*

As an Internet advertising expert told me once, "The web is the ultimate repository of specific, quality resources if you know what you're looking for."

THE INTERNET UPSIDES AND DOWNSIDES

If you view the Internet from a business perspective and not a lifestyle perspective (games, downloads, video, sports, and so on), you'll find that there are social media platforms but no *business media platforms.* Moreover, the ability to create communities of followers and supporters varies widely on a progression.

---

* We talk about this in our book *Million Dollar Web Presence*, Entrepreneur Press, 2012.

You begin on the left with what is, in effect, a vanity press operation in Facebook, continue toward the middle in public but specialized sites such as Monster.com, and finally arrive at business-specific sites such as my AlansForums.com.

You have to be highly discriminating on the Internet; Facebook is like a party with the door left open and Alan's Forums is like an elite club where membership is by invitation only.

What kind of relationship do you want to create with prospects and clients?

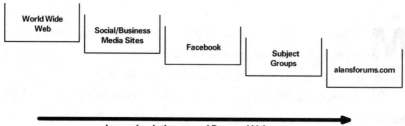

A progression from public/generic to private/specific

The upside of the Internet is:

- The ability to reach global audiences daily, in real time or by time-shifting.

- Enabling people to readily find you and understand your value and credibility.

- Passive product sales.

- Testimonials and other materials in multimedia.

- Creation of an archive or repository of high-quality content and expertise.

- Rapid response potential.

> ## Launch Lesson
> *Start with a modest site with your value, typical client results, and testimonials. Have someone else create it. You need an expert, not a professional consultant who's a web-design amateur.*

The downside of the Internet is:

- It's a distraction, with everything from too much e-mail to surfing allure.
- You can't retrieve or do a mulligan* on an inappropriate e-mail you've sent.
- You can be lost in a great sea of mediocrity.
- Technical problems can cost you time, money, and effectiveness.
- The safety and storage of information are always concerns.

There are far more dramatic upsides than trivial downsides, and its value is immense if you control the way you utilize cyberspace. Here are some basic rules:

1. Find inexpensive alternatives for your basic needs. You might not need both a desktop and a laptop computer, and perhaps can get by with only a notebook computer. Make intelligent judgments about your needs. (Example: I'm a writer, so I need a heavy-duty keyboard and sophisticated word processing.)
2. Never let the technology interrupt you or control your time. Turn off notifications, and don't allow the computer to indicate when e-mail has arrived. Proceed with your daily schedule without interruption.

---

* A second shot in golf when the initial shot was poor.

3. Start your website simple and don't invest too much at the outset.

4. Do blog frequently on your expertise.

5. Rigidly discriminate between your recreational and even educational needs and your business use. Angry Birds is not good practice for dealing with buyers, no matter how much you rationalize.

6. Don't worry about matching every URL with your company and/ or brand. I use Alan's Blog, which is on ContrarianConsulting .com and is owned by Summit Consulting Group, Inc. However, do *not* use ridiculous e-mail addresses: alanwhoisnumberone@ themeetingwarrior-Phoenix-from-ashes.org.

7. Back up your data intelligently, on a platform such as Dropbox, and stop pursuing 23 backups that would allow you to resurface and do business on Jupiter if the Earth exploded.

Script

Self-script: How can I quickly create a website and blog at minimal expense that will express my value, results, testimonials, and expertise? Who can do this for me flexibly and with excellent responsiveness?

HOW TO CREATE AND EXPLOIT A GREAT BLOG

I blog about five times a week, even at this stage of my career. I differentiate blogs from social media platforms because *your blog is your personal business media platform.* You can see my blog's banner on the facing page.

Alan's Blog banner

The URL for my blog is contrarianconsulting.com, but it's called Alan's Blog. The ultimate brand is your name.

> ### Launch Lesson
> *Don't worry about matching brand, URL, site names, and so on. Just ensure that your name is prominently displayed on everything you create, publish, and circulate.*

Blogs *should be* somewhat idiosyncratic. They should reflect your personality as well as your beliefs, values, insights, suggestions, IP, experiences, and so forth. For example, here are the categories currently on my blog:

- Alan's Monday Morning Memo
- Alan's Quest
- Alan's Thought For Today
- Alanisms
- Alas, Babylon
- Announcements
- Business of Consulting
- Consulting Opportunities
- Consulting Philosophy
- DASM
- Guest Column
- In Case You Were Wondering What I Was Thinking

- It's Not Your Mother's Fault
- King of Social Media
- Marketing Examples
- Peregrinations
- Personal Improvement
- Podcast Series: The Way I See It
- Podcasts Series: Brave New World
- The Best of Life
- The Critic
- The Dog Star
- The Friday Funnies
- The Good Ones
- The Movies
- The Movies: Life in Reel Time
- The Movies: The Writing on the Wall

I include everything from cartoons (for which I hire an artist to portray my stories about my dogs) to video, from podcasts to reviews, from business advice to social commentary.

Perhaps *the* most important points about your blogging are:

1. *Frequency:* Blog a minimum of three-to-five times a week. The posts can be short paragraphs and quick insights.

2. *Responsiveness:* Unlike newsletters, blogs *should be* interactive. One thing I do is allow, encourage, and respond to commentary. This is a major drawing point and stimulator for a viral dynamic. Get into debates and discussions with your readers.

3. *Perspective: Never* pay attention to traffic, hits, or other quantitative nonsense. Don't worry about unsolicited critiques. Just focus on consistently providing value, allowing your personality to shine through, and being responsive. You only need one hit every so often that provides business.

Mention your clients when you can—with permission, of course—and use graphics and photos as much as possible. You can become an object of interest on the Internet with an intelligent, provocative, pragmatic blog.

Options such as WordPress provide ideal templates to quickly set up and administer a blog without paying someone else to do so. (If you have the cash, it's often easier and always less time consuming to allow a third party to take care of technical issues.)

I'm contrarian in suggesting that you do *not* embed your blog in your website, but rather use a completely different URL address to maximize your exposure and focus people on your outreach efforts. Blogs are too often lost in links or on drop-down menus on websites.

Blogging is an inexpensive way to market whenever the spirit moves you and is a fundamental component of your digital-empire building. Make sure you include your blog address in your e-mail signature file, stationery, website, and any other places you have contact information.

THE TRUTH ABOUT SOCIAL MEDIA

The fates know that by the time you read this there could be 14 more digital revolutions and holographic imaging is taking over communications.

Your intention is to acquire business for your professional services practice within 90 days of launch. If you're targeting the corporate (wholesale) world, you should avoid social media except for recreation and entertainment. There is always an exception, and there are 100,000 social media "marketing experts" who will tell you otherwise, but corporate buyers do not buy based on social media appearances.

They may go to LinkedIn or Facebook to find out something about you if they've heard of you elsewhere, but they're more likely to visit your website and/or blog (a website is a credibility tool, not a sales tool). They will have heard of you through the platinum standard (peer-level reference), gold standard (commercially published book), or silver standard (word of mouth, speeches, public presence).

A book is generally out of the question in the first 90 days, and a public presence takes time, which is why I've emphasized the power of referrals and creating personal contacts immediately. The danger is that *you waste precious time on social media sites, convincing yourself you're engaged in marketing.*

Here's a comparison that may be of interest:

If people visit LinkedIn twice a day for 15 minutes each time, that's two-and-a-half hours in a five-day week. (I'm discounting weekends, though I shouldn't, because social media wandering is clearly a full-time avocation, but I want to be conservative here.) If they visit Facebook four times a day for 10 minutes each, that's roughly three-and-a-third hours. If they're on Twitter six times a day for five minutes each time, that two-and-a-half hours (or 12 times at two-and-a-half minutes each—you get the idea).

Drum roll, please: We now have a five-day week on a conventional 40-hour basis with about 10 hours engaged in what is somewhat inappropriately termed social media. I understand that those hours may well extend into evening or early morning time. On the basis of a 40-hour week, that's 25 percent devoted to this stuff.

If you were devoting about half of those 13 hours—say, six hours—to other professional marketing pursuits, I estimate you could do any one of the following during that week:

- Create and post 10–12 position papers on your website.
- Call, at a moderate pace with follow-up, 30 past clients and/or warm leads.
- Send out a dozen press releases.
- Engage in a full day of self-development or a workshop.
- Create three speeches or a complete multiday workshop.
- Create a new product to be sold on your website.
- Create and develop a marketing plan for a teleconference.

- Create and record three podcasts.

- Create and tape a video.

- Contact 30 prior contacts for testimonials, referrals, or references.

- Attend two networking events.

- Create and distribute two newsletters.

- Respond to 50 or more reporters' inquiries on, say, PRLeads.com.

- Seek out two high-potential pro bono opportunities.

- Contact and follow up with five trade associations for speaking opportunities.

Launch Lesson

The best marketing tools are seldom the easiest or to be found on the path of least resistance. It's better to face your fears of rejection by calling a prospect for an appointment than it is to fool yourself about the acceptance of the denizens on Facebook.

If you're launching a consumer (retail) service operation, social media will no doubt be more helpful. You can find contacts, form groups, promote yourself, request testimonials, and so forth. I would think that a couple of hours of serious research and promotion might well be worth it. But you'll also be deluged with reciprocal requests from people who want things from you.

Thus, even on the consumer side, the more traditional marketing is far more likely to garner you business within your first 90 days at a far less labor-intensive and intrusive manner. Right now, Facebook is a huge vanity press, with people proclaiming their favorite platitudes, displaying photos of their latest testimonial letter (or fourth-grade report card), and occasionally acting as though they're at a bad Boston bar at closing—noisy, loud, and drunk.

LinkedIn is a job-seekers warehouse, with people requesting endorsements from others not vaguely familiar with their work or quality and willing to return the somewhat unethical favor. Twitter is the equivalent of texting what you're having for breakfast.

Yes, there are exceptions. And, yes, I'm on all three or I wouldn't be credible in commenting on their worth. But how do you want to spend your very valuable time in trying to acquire business in your first three months?

Script

High-level people discuss results, low-level people, deliverables. (One of my typical tweets to provide value quickly.)

THE REAL ESTATE OF YOUR WEBSITE

If you've been planning your new venture prior to launch, or if you have friends who can help quickly, you probably have a website in place or in mind. My view on websites is different from that of technology people and even from most marketers.

I believe a website for *corporate consultants* is a credibility statement, not a sales tool. And the most important credibility—just as in a speech, article, book, or introduction—is the immediate and first impression.

Hence, you should view a website home page as real estate:

- Is it attractive?
- Is it well kept and uncluttered?

- Would other people like to live in this neighborhood?

- Does its value increase over time?

- Is it distinctive?

- Is it aesthetically pleasing?

- Can you find your way around easily?

- Is there a central point of focus and attention?

Here are some of my favorite site home pages as of this writing:

> http://libbywagner.com
> http://www.wilkersonconsulting.net
> http://sethgodin.com/sg
> http://visionaryleadership.com/site
> http://setiliandassociates.com

You'll note that they display the personality of the principal clearly, provide specific benefits or results for the reader, and favor testimonials. Seth Godin's site isn't as strong on these because he has such a robust brand and following, so he can be a minimalist and simply invite people in. I've included him to show that evolution.

The others are people who I have mentored, and who have developed powerful yet diverse businesses in the corporate and nonprofit marketplaces. At launch, or very quickly thereafter, a strong home page with very simple support is more than sufficient. On the home page, feature:

- Your photo

- Testimonials, preferably some of which are brief videos of no more than one minute. These can rotate to make the best use of real estate.*

---

* Use at least eight seconds for each rotation, so that people have time to read them.

- Typical client results. These are outcomes, not deliverables, and are typical, not specific to a client engagement. Feel free to create what they might be.

- Clear contact information, by e-mail, phone, and physical address. Don't make people search for it or leave their e-mail address in order to obtain it.

Support pages can feature:

- Position papers on your intellectual property.
- Biographical sketch.
- Case studies (also typical and created by you).
- Further testimonials
- Your blog or a link to your blog (I prefer a separate web address for blogs).

A website is organic, growing over time. Don't be obsessed with a complete site, because, like San Simeon, it's never going to be completely complete. The home page is the absolute key, now and forever. I like my site to be a cul de sac, so I don't include links that take people elsewhere. I don't want to send them away for any reason.

> **Launch Lesson**
>
> *You don't have to have a website to launch your practice. But it's rather simple to put up a professional home page with a few powerful basics and fill in the rest later.*

Whatever you do with your site, *do not* put up an under-construction sign or indicate it's coming soon. Either don't have a site at all or have one with a professional home page. The under-construction approach screams amateur or broken.

Don't feel you need to artificially hype yourself. Including photos and résumés of people who might work with you on a subcontractual basis is a bad idea. People are seeking your value and your expertise, and your credibility should be based on that: typical results (what's in it for the reader) and testimonials (who says so).

A word about testimonials: You're thinking, "I don't have any yet. I'm just starting out and you're supposed to be telling me how to get business! If I *had* business and testimonials, I wouldn't need you!"

Here's how to get testimonials as soon as you launch, or even before.

1. Solicit *character* testimonials from those who know you well and who have significant positions: lawyers, bank managers, doctors, accounting firm partners, and so on.

2. Speak for free at service clubs and chambers of commerce. When someone says they enjoyed your talk, ask for a written (electronic or hard copy) testimonial. It will come on their letterhead, and you'll have a testimonial from a manager at Metropolitan Life without claiming that they're a client.

3. Use a video camera or smartphone to record (these are excellent for impromptu testimonials) kind words when the situation is appropriate.

Always get written permission to use text or video testimonials.

Script 1

I'm so happy you enjoyed my four points on customer referrals and how to stimulate them. Since referrals are the coinage of my realm, might I have that in writing or on video to help with future clients?

> **Script 2**
>
> *I'm starting a new practice and, as my attorney, I wonder if you'd be kind enough to give me a brief testimonial on my ethics, character, follow through, and similar traits you've observed? This would be of immense help in beginning my marketing work.*

WHEN HIGH TOUCH TRUMPS HIGH TECH

John Naisbitt, in his seminal book, *Megatrends,* wrote in 1982 that we were entering the world of "high tech/high touch," meaning that the more we used technology, the more we'd also need to emphasize the interrelationships that support our lives through other people.

He was absolutely right, one of the few prognosticators who got something exactly right. Until recently.

Today, high tech enables high touch. While high tech can still inappropriately supplant high touch—as in the infuriating menu systems and automated responses of credit card companies, banks, and other uncaring institutions—it more often can heighten and amplify it.

For example, as you are reading this paragraph, people from all over the world are visiting AlansForums.com and exchanging views on ethics, marketing, fees, personal development, sales, delivery, and so forth. My membership-only forums provide real-time and time-shifted responses. Technology is enabling personal contact on a more flexible and global basis than ever before. We have over 150,000 posts as of this writing.

Why is this important to you in the first three months (or to anyone in service professions at any time)? Because this is a:

1. *Marketing business:* We have to identify or create a need that we can fulfill to be successful in acquiring business.

2. *Relationship business:* We sell to individuals, and a trusting relationship is key to the conversion from prospect to client.

Therefore, technology makes sense early on in your dealings *insofar as it augments and accelerates the relationship.*

Again: E-mail is one dimensional. The phone is two dimensional. Personal contact is three dimensional. Technology can marry these to create superior relationships and more rapid decision making.

Examples:

- You can deliver a proposal within hours of a conversation by submitting it electronically.

- You can establish customized value for a client or prospect on special website pages.

- You can publish a blog post at any hour on any day of any length, including text, audio, video, graphics, photos, and so forth.

- You can create automated, tailored newsletters with subscription, change of address, and unsubscribe functions that you don't have to administer.

- You can send links and items of interest embedded in or attached to e-mail.

- You can deliver or facilitate teleconferences and webinars with questions and answers taking place in real time online.

- Options such as Skype or Virtual Office allow you to interact in real time over the Internet as though the other party were next to you. You can do so with groups as well.

- Software such as Dropbox or Evernote allow you to maintain records on multiple platforms, which update immediately as any one file is updated (this sentence, for example, will be present on my iPad, iPhone, and laptop as I write it on my desktop computer).

- You can stay in touch no matter where you are via smartphone or with Wi-Fi services in hotels, on airplanes, or elsewhere (and with cards from carriers such as Verizon).

Launch Lesson

Use technology to enhance your interpersonal and relationship dealings, not replace them. What people expect these days isn't instant access but rapid responsiveness.

In your position, I would use technology to:

- Collect messages and return all calls within two hours (my own standard is 90 minutes) and all e-mail within four hours, during business hours.
- Provide value, background material, examples, visuals, and so on to prospects upon request.
- Create a follow-on procedure to ensure that the date/time/action sequence is pursued with discipline for every lead and contact. These are the lifeblood of your early launch.
- Create a distinctive online presence on the home page of your website, blog, and/or newsletter.
- Deliver instant proposals within hours of the conversation.
- Promote your services and value in e-mail signature files, blog margins, and website testimonials.
- Acquire and display video testimonials. Here's a superb 90-second video from one of my coaching clients, Amanda Setili: http://setiliandassociates.com/main/sharing-our-thinking/videos/setili-in–90-seconds/.

Let's turn now to a more aggressive pursuit of ideal prospects while we're still in the first 60 days.

Script

Thanks for calling. Please leave your name and phone number, even if you think we already have it, at the beep. Please repeat it slowly, and I'll get back to you within two hours during normal business hours. (That's it: no one cares where you are or what your thought is for the day!)

6

PURSUING THE IDEAL PROSPECT

Not all prospects are equal, and you need to focus on those who are of the highest potential during the first three months. These will be successful people at successful companies who have a history and willingness to invest in external help and resources. We're heading into the last part of the second two months.

THE MARKET VALUE BELL CURVE

I spoke earlier about finding your ideal buyer. Remember, you don't conduct business with entities, no matter whether it's GE or the dry cleaner down the block. You deal with people in those enterprises, and the key person for you is that person who can sign a check in return for your value—whether a senior manager in a large company or the owner of a small one.

If you believe everyone is your prospect, then no one is your prospect (just as if everything is a priority, nothing is a priority). I've created a schematic to help you understand who your ideal buyers really are so that you can hone in on them in your marketing and relationships, as well as inform others as to who constitutes the best referrals to your business.

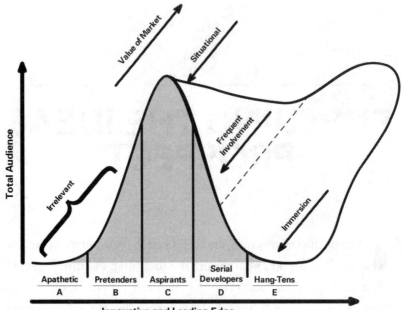

Market value bell curve

Above you can see that the distinction is the third dimension. That is, this is more than a two-dimensional depiction. It has depth, which you can see on the right side.

On the left are those people who are apathetic or irrelevant to your value. They are nonbuyers (low level) or not appropriate (public educators when your value is for large companies, or vice versa). In the middle are fence sitters who could become buyers but would require substantial persuasion.

You can't afford that time in the first 90 days.

Thus, on the right, you have the serial developers, who believe in consistent growth and improvement for their people (and themselves) and the hang 10, from the surfing term for willingness to take risks to create excitement and a great ride (hanging ten toes over the edge of the board). Note that third dimension.

Launch Lesson

You're better off with a smaller number of highly qualified and relevant prospects than with a universe of the uninformed, unenlightened, and uninterested.

You want to try to penetrate those populations on the right-hand side of the chart. That means you need to identify who they are. For example, if your expertise is in more effective phone communications and your value proposition is to improve the number and size of sales through telemarketing, you may have these criteria for your ideal buyers:

- Senior sales managers of telemarketing groups

- Senior sales managers of field sales groups who also use the phone to acquire appointments

- Managers and directors of call center operations, where complaints can be used to upsell

- Managers and directors of repair and service functions, where requests for assistance can also be used to upsell

- Senior managers in charge of providing and extending warrantees, guarantees, and contracts

You get the idea. Note that particular industries aren't terribly important, because your skills are *process* skills and can be used with auto dealers, appliance centers, insurance sales, catalog operations, and so on. In a smaller business market, you may be looking for the owner or general manager. In a nonprofit, you may need the development director or the executive director.

Once you can identify and begin to list those on the right side, you can attract their attention. But first you *must* develop this clear idea of who it is you're seeking and want to attract. Otherwise, you're going to waste precious time on nonbuyers and the uninterested, and I've seen professional service providers waste a year on this, let alone the first three months.

No matter who you are and what you do, within these parameters, your ideal buyer will have the authority and funds to purchase, a history or willingness to use external resources, and a need that either exists or that you can readily create.

Let's see how that comes about.

Script

Self-script: What type of economic buyer, responsible for what results in his or her enterprise, would be most likely to have need for my value or most readily appreciate the need that I express?

STREAMS YOU ENTER AND STREAMS YOU CREATE

Your prospective buyers have streams of influence that help determine their decisions and preferences. Once you know who your ideal buyers are on the right side of the Market Value Bell Curve, you can identify their most likely streams of influence.

In general, the most powerful stream of influence is peer-to-peer direct referral. Think about this, and it's not very surprising. How do you choose vacation sites, movies, restaurants, or computers? You may read reviews and advertising, but you are most powerfully influenced by people you trust who have had the experience you seek.

I ask a technology expert I know which camera I should buy for my purposes, and I simply follow his advice without question.* I read

---

* A callout to Alex Goldfayn at Evangelist Marketing and The Technology Tailor: http://www .evangelistmktg.com.

about car choice and visit showrooms, but I listen most closely to people with similar demands for a car who have purchased and driven them. There are some people who will recommend a book or movie and I'll immediately read or see it (and others who cause me to run the other way).

You're probably quite similar, because this is the major stream in influencing buying decisions. Hence, executives, managers, and owners are subject to similar persuasion when making business and professional decisions. (Hinge Marketing has done some fascinating studies and surveys about this topic.)

Consequently, many people waste their time—even if they've found the ideal buyer—on direct mail and cold calls, which have virtually no influence in the sale of professional services. And in your case, with the goal of business within 90 days, you can't take the time for these laborious, time-consuming measures anyway. So how do you enter the most powerful streams of influence?

First, meticulously find contacts who know people who know people. Remember, it's about people, not entities. Don't seek to "get into Boeing," seek to find someone who knows someone who knows the manager you want to meet—your ideal buyer. (Your ideal buyer in large firms is virtually never the CEO. There are scores, if not hundreds, of buyers in complex corporations.) If you seek these introductions boldly, meticulously working your way upward (and never settling for a low-level contact), you'll meet the key people within 60 days or less.

Second, get in front of recommenders. Speak wherever you can, even for free. Just be sure there are influencers in the audience. Offer pro bono work to a nonprofit that has recommenders (or buyers) on the board and among the donors. Offer media interviews on your expertise. Host a breakfast or other event. (This takes about six weeks for invitations and delivery, so you can do it well within the 90 days. But it's imperative that you understand your ideal buyer before inviting anyone.)

> **Launch Lesson**
>
> *Start calling people the minute you know you're going out on your own, with the intention of finding routes to the influencers of your key buyers. If you're afraid to do this or feel you're intruding, then look for a nine-to-five job, because this one isn't for you.*

Third, make sure every professional contact you have knows what your new venture is and your specific value. These are people who, as a normal part of their careers, serve as peer influencers. They would include:

- *Attorneys:* estate, litigation, contract, even divorce (a silver lining in a past cloud)

- *Finance:* CPAs, accountants, tax professionals, bankers, insurance brokers and agents, investment professionals, and bookkeepers

- *Doctors and dentists:* pediatric, geriatric, primary care, surgeons, dermatologists, orthodontists, and cosmetic surgeons

- *Home care:* landscapers, interior designers, plumbers, electricians, carpenters, and painters*

- *Clubs and activities:* managers, chefs, schedulers, executive directors, artistic directors, and development directors

- *Charities:* board members, major donors, executive staff, prominent volunteers, and sponsors

You get the idea. You can enter these streams through careful selection and then willpower. Formally (in presentations) and informally

---

* These blue-collar professionals very often provide ideas and suggestions to their wealthy customers.

(in conversations and networking), mention your value and your venture, ask for advice and introductions. If you think this is unreasonable in some way, I'd remind you that auto sales, insurance, and realty—to name just three—are businesses that rely almost entirely on these practices.

Finally, you can actually become the stream of influence yourself. Although this is easiest in the longer term and beyond 90 days, you can begin early by writing op-ed pieces in the newspaper, taking contrarian and controversial stands on relevant topics for your expertise, and pursuing leveraged platforms. (In other words, don't just tell the club manager what you're doing, ask the club to sponsor an enrichment evening during which you provide free value for interested members after dinner one evening.)

When you become the stream, you no longer require middlemen.

Script

Jerry, I know your company has been doing business with Acme Widget, and I'd love to meet their general manager. If you don't know him personally, could you introduce me to your Acme sales representative so that I could pursue it with her?

DELIVERING WHILE MARKETING, MARKETING WHILE DELIVERING

There is an ancient rubric in professional services that you can't market (let alone sell) while delivering, and you can't deliver while you market. That makes sense only if you view life as one huge on/off switch and you've never seen a rheostat.

The better you deliver, especially at this early stage of the game, the better you can market within that account, so long as you do so from the standpoint of a helping hand and valued partner. People will be impressed with your work, and your responses might include:

- Here's what might make an even greater impact
- You need to do this as well, and you may choose to do it yourself or with my help
- This is a process, not an event, and you'll want to keep this active and supported
- Your people are highly motivated; you'll want to maintain that momentum
- Would you like me to create leverage by including your other areas and/or other people?
- There are ways to gain back even more on this investment
- People have been asking me if I can also help with *X*, so I'd like to run that by you
- There would be huge economies of scale in expanding this

Launch Lesson

If your attitude is one of providing more and more value to improve the client's condition, neither you nor the client will view suggestions as intrusions, but rather as added benefits to consider.

Please bear in mind two equally invidious aspects to this, which occur when you *don't* charge extra fees for extra value:

1. *Scope creep:* The client (or client's people) ask you to do what you suggest or they suggest as part of the project. This is an attempt, maliciously or inadvertently, to extract more of your talent at no investment.

2. *Scope seep: You* suggest that you perform additional work to deliver more value for free in an insecure attempt to justify your fee out of concern the client won't see you as worth the investment.

If you become entangled in these webs, you'll never be able to market while you deliver because you'll be on a treadmill of delivery, never escaping, despite your feeble shouts of "Help me!"

Never be loath to suggest new value to your buyer, because providing new value to existing clients, where trust already exists, is one of the best and shortest-term ways to create additional business.

Case Study

I was working with a very large bank's domestic senior management when I noticed someone I had never met sitting in the back of the room. I asked who he was and was informed he was the visiting head of European operations.

I introduced myself later and told him I suspected that not one thing I was doing with his colleagues *couldn't* be applicable to Europe. He asked for a description and proposal and became a "new" client that week.

What about delivering while you're marketing? That's more than merely the converse.

You can market passively even when you're fully engaged with delivery for any number of clients. Focus on:

- Having website articles that can be downloaded
- Timing blog posts to automatically appear in your "absence"
- Create a few promotional lines for the signature file of your e-mail
- Use video testimonials on your digital offerings

- Create downloads of audio (podcasts/teleconferences) that can be accessed on iTunes
- Create downloads of video that can be accessed on YouTube
- Make your calls and send e-mail during breaks, lunch, in the morning or in the evening

Example: My service standard is to return all calls within 90 minutes during business hours (U.S. eastern time). Even when I'm fully engaged in delivering a workshop or a strategy session, I can call in at 10:30, noon, 2:30, and 4. These represent breaks, lunch, and the usual end of my workday on-site. People no longer expect to immediately reach you by phone (which is why you don't have to provide your cell number and usually shouldn't, if you want to control your time), and they're delighted to receive prompt, promised responses.

Don't allow yourself to ride the bipolar roller coaster, in which you're depressed when you have too little business because you're not making much money, and depressed when you get a lot of business because you're afraid you won't be able to market with all that delivery and will continue to alternate between feast and famine.

Pursue your ideal prospects at all times, even while working with them. This is not a scheduled or sometime event. It's a continual process because *you and I are in the marketing business and happen to be consultants, or designers, or coaches, or architects, or whatever.* And when you're comfortable enough to streamline your delivery, the equation becomes even simpler.

Script

Ted, at this point I often find my most successful clients want to institutionalize their success and guarantee that it continues perpetually. Would you like to talk about some options that would allow me to help you accomplish that?

WHY ANY PARTNERSHIP WILL WORK AGAINST YOU

I assume the counterintuitive title of this segment may have gained your attention. I hope so, because I'm about to save you an enormous amount of time, accelerate your initial business acquisition, and enable you to avoid some horrible relationships.

Logically—and certainly emotionally—it appears to make sense to join forces with others, especially at the beginning of your career. One would think that the whole is greater than the sum of its parts: you're gaining capabilities, acquiring more contacts, obtaining commiseration and support.

You're not.

Virtually all ideas about and attempts at partnership and collaboration and alliances are strictly conceptual (even for veterans, many years into their careers). That's because there's both safety and solace in sitting around a table with a glass of wine making theoretical plans about how the two of you would work together, deliver projects, and apportion business.

Except there is no business.

What you're actually talking about is a conceptual framework that won't hold when needed and, worse, probably will never be needed. The whole isn't greater than the sum of the parts. Clients rarely see the advantages you do; prospects don't care. (If you are asked by another firm to take on a small piece of business within your expertise, that's called subcontracting, not a partnership, and you'll be paid by the hour, like a waiter, but without the tips.)

Remember the movie *Jerry Maguire*, in which the actor Cuba Gooding, Jr., kept demanding, "Show me the money"? That's the operative question here. If someone else comes to you with grand plans to collaborate and form an alliance, ask, "Where's the money?" ("Where's the business?") Without specific business on the table, all ensuing discussions are like planning what you'll have for dinner in Rome when you have no reservations, plane tickets, vacation time, or passport.

There will be no nutrition.

On the other hand, as all hedging economists are fond of saying, if *you* have business that *you* believe requires assistance to close, then you have the money to show the person whom you need. (If you simply need help to deliver it, then *you* pay someone by the hour to do so. Hire a waiter.)

In the unlikely event—that is, unlikely in the first 90 days—that you do find yourself in this position, there's a formula below that will save major portions of your life:

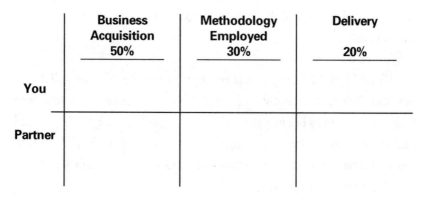

	Business Acquisition 50%	**Methodology Employed** 30%	**Delivery** 20%
You			
Partner			

Alliance apportionment

I've identified three parts of the obtaining and execution of business: acquisition, methodology, and delivery.

Acquisition: The finding and conversion of a lead into business.*

Methodology: The techniques, approaches, and technology required to create the changes needed to meet the client's objectives for that project.

Delivery: The physical provision of the intervention, which is often in person but may also be provided via technology (e.g., distance learning, surveys, electronic schematics, and so on).

---

* You can pay a finder's fee for a lead that turns into business when someone else makes an introduction, but that's not our topic here.

Note that there are three elements, but they are not equally important. I've assigned 50 percent of the credit to the acquisition, 30 percent to the methodology employed, and 20 percent to the actual delivery.

Let's take a $100,000 project. If I were to find it and close it, I would earn $50,000 of the total. If we used your methodology, which is why I needed you as a partner, you would earn $30,000. And if we shared equally in the delivery, we would each earn $10,000.

Hence: You earn $40,000 and I earn $60,000. I call this objective apportionment because it's based on an objective assessment of what the elements are worth and who is contributing exactly what. Never let people who strictly deliver tell you they are the ultimate quality factor and the most important piece. These people—sorry to be harsh—are a dime a dozen. They're good at delivery but can't market (remember I said this is the *marketing* business), so they can solely deliver. Consequently, there are a lot of them out there and they don't command a high fee.

Bear in mind that this last 60/40 example is the only true partnership or alliance I've mentioned. And it clearly occurs only when you have a project, know the fee, and can talk pragmatically in real time about who does what and when.

Otherwise, you're simply writing fiction.

In the initial three months, a true partnership is an exceedingly unlikely scenario, so *don't* waste time sitting around discussing what might have been when it will likely never be.

Script

I appreciate your interest in my work and offer of help, but I'm very busy marketing and gaining my own appointments, so unless you have specific business you'd like to discuss with me, I'll have to pass on your kind offer.

WHOLESALE AND RETAIL*

In the wholesale market, a buyer who makes the decisions will generally include intervention beyond himself or herself (although not always, as in a coaching project for the buyer personally). Nevertheless, the project is paid for with a corporate check. This includes the owner of a closely held business.[†]

In the retail market, the individual is purchasing for himself or herself, and the buyer is the consumer, client, or customer looking for a personal benefit. This buyer is generally easier to reach and is often more of an impulse buyer.

I wanted to end this chapter on ideal prospects by ensuring that you understand that your prospects may be wholesale, retail, or a combination of both. Examples:

- Attorneys can represent individuals or corporations.
- Consultants can advise both.
- Coaches may work with individuals or enterprises.
- Realtors work with either.
- Accountants work with either.
- Designers can work with either.
- Large consultancies work solely with organizations.
- Search firms and recruiters work solely with organizations.
- Venture capitalists focus solely on enterprises.
- Dentists and oral surgeons work only with individuals.
- Tax preparers work solely with individuals.

---

* Wholesale refers to corporate sales, with a buyer spending money on behalf of the organization, while retail refers to individual sales, with a consumer spending money for himself or herself.

[†] I'm refraining from using the phrase *small business*, since it means different things to different people. The mom-and-pop operation may go up to $250 million or more in revenue and beyond.

You get the idea. You may choose to work with one or the other, but be aware of your options. The key criteria include:

1. Can the buyer—an individual or a corporate manager—make the decision alone (e.g., is this a true buyer)?
2. Can that buyer pay your fee?
3. Can you minimize labor intensity?

Personally, I've worked exclusively with the wholesale market, then a combination of wholesale and retail, and now almost solely with retail. If you've purchased this book from McGraw-Hill, from Amazon, from a bookstore, from my website, or some similar source, *you* are a retail customer representing passive income.

In the next chapter we'll discuss the Million Dollar Consulting Accelerant Curve, and you'll be able to create offerings that appeal to either or both, and that may be passive or require your active intervention. These are choices that people often stumble upon or realize years after beginning their business. I'm advising you to make some proactive, early choices about *what value you want to provide to whom.*

Launch Lesson

You do not have to specialize, not only among types of businesses, but even within a given market. "Specialize or die" is the biggest myth since refraining from swimming for an hour after you eat.

On the market value bell curve introduced at the beginning of this chapter, we talked about the ideal prospects.

You can create this for retail and wholesale clients, and I suggest you do so for each if you're intent on marketing to each, because the ideal buyers on the right side will obviously be different.

Your website is a credibility statement for the wholesale buyer, for example, but can be a sales platform for the retail buyer, featuring booklets, audio, video, subscriptions, and so on as your career progresses. You can see my retail bookstore online here: http://summitconsulting.com/store and my relevance to corporate entities here: http://summitconsulting.com/services/consulting.php

Thus, on your site, in your networking, during your conversations, in your writing, and as part of your general marketing, you should include appeals to whatever segment you're intent on attracting. For any advisory professionals (coaches, financial experts, consultants, investment specialists, event planners) the ability to successfully operate in both segments is generally easier.

Your priority is to appear on the radar screens of those buyers who populate the right side of the Market Value Bell Curve, whether corporate, individual, or both.

Script

Self-script: Would I prefer to work with individual clients who are more plentiful but will average smaller fees, or with corporate entities that may be harder to attract but represent far higher individual fees and probably more complex projects?

PART II REVIEW

After 30 days, you should be learning the lay of the land, which means that you should have your bearings about what the early sources of help have and *have not* been.

IS IT YOU OR IS IT THEM?

There are people who will tell you early on that they will help—with contacts, resources, suggestions, and so forth. These may range from direct referrals or even offers of providing business, to access to office space or financial terms. However, talk is cheap, and relatively few people have actually done what you've done (or are considering): actually begin a new professional services practice in a methodical, intelligent manner.

Thus, a lot of people make promises they feel they will never be called upon to deliver.

You need to find out now, in the second month, if you haven't already, who is going to come through for you. The question might be, "Joan, you said I could use one of the empty offices in your law firm to meet with prospects. I'm ready to do so. Which office is available on Wednesday, the 14th?" Or you may remind someone, "Jim, you offered to give me access to your database to solicit subscriptions for my new newsletter. My own site is up and running and my first edition can go out immediately. How can we arrange access to your list?"

If you find you're welcomed, as promised, then charge ahead. But if you find that "the time isn't right" or "get back to me in a couple of months," just move on. Don't hold grudges or become disillusioned. But, above all, don't waste time trying to cash in on empty promises.

So, by the beginning of the second month, be very clear what resource promises and commitments you can count on and begin using them, and disregard the disingenuous.

This leads to a second, more painful examination. Are *you* proceeding according to your own promises?

Here's an exercise that might make sense if you're unsure whether or not you're meeting your own commitments to yourself. Several of my veteran coaching clients still use it to this day.

First, write down no more than four things you'd like to accomplish in the next week. For example:

1. Make five calls for referrals

2. Send out two inquiries to write articles

3. Visit a former colleague who may have worked for me

4. Finalize the four initial pages of my website and launch

Second, at the end of the week, record actual progress. For example:

1. Made three calls for referrals

2. Sent out two inquiries

3. Colleague requested reschedule for next week

4. Website launched per plan

Finally, write why things worked or didn't work, and complete the next week's priorities. For example:

1. Didn't get around to all five because they weren't in my calendar. I'll do five this week but schedule them, one per day.

2. I had scheduled these. I'll send out two more and follow up on the first two.

3. This was a legitimate request, since he was called out of town unexpectedly, but I will call two days prior to new date to reconfirm. If he doesn't accept or reschedules again, I'll cross this off my prospect list. There is one other colleague who may be of help whom I'll call tomorrow.

4. I had talked to the web designer twice, and will now set a goal with him of launching a simple blog within the week.

This is a systematic, disciplined way to ensure that *you* aren't undermining yourself. It's self-accountability that you can enforce at the conclusion of every week. And I do find that even seasoned professionals find it helpful throughout their careers.

COLLECTING MONEY

We're organized here to help you gain business rapidly, which means you should be prepared to collect money rapidly. In the initial 30 days, any success you have with former employers and/or immediate referral sources should be literally paying off by now. Perhaps you received a deposit or advance payment, but you may have waited because many companies' systems don't pay until at least 30 days after an agreement is reached.

Let's examine some basic procedures in detail that may bear frequent consideration.

Terms

Your terms should always call for payment on agreement or commencement for small projects. These may include a speech, or a day of coaching, or a brief analysis, or feedback of any kind. Sometimes you will have to wait while payment is "processed," but at the end of 30 days, if you aren't paid, you should go to your buyer and say, "We have a problem: my payment hasn't been received per our agreement."

Never argue with accounts payable, or purchasing, or procurement, or other strangers in the organization. Go back to your buyer and ask for help with *our* problem.

Never accept payment terms of, say, net 90 days, which means the agreement is not to pay for your 90 days and you may well not be paid for 120 days. If your payments are in installments for larger projects, treat each installment as I have indicated with single payments.

With small companies (legal offices, start-ups, real estate agencies, insurance brokerages, franchise owners) you may find the excuse that there are "cash flow problems." That may well be, but that's not *your* problem. You're a small business deserving to be paid per the terms of the agreement. *Note: If you accept these excuses, you will be placed at the bottom of the priority list for payment because it is now known that you will agree to wait, so the effects are cumulative.* Banks don't wait for mortgage payments; they make it clear they should be top priority.

So should you.

Expense Reimbursement

If you find that you have to spend your own money on travel, meals, tips, lodging, and so on (but not supplies or postage or phone), submit your expenses *promptly*. Don't allow these to build up or, aside from not collecting them rapidly, the client may scrutinize them even more closely if they're very late, delaying the reimbursement still further.

Submit expenses in a detailed manner, with any receipts that are required, on the last day of the month, with your invoice marked "Due on presentation" or "Due on receipt." Again, never provide terms such as net 30 or you'll be waiting at least 60 days or more for repayment. And at this point in your career, cash flow is vital.

If you have challenges periodically paying your own bills, my suggestion is to always pay local merchants first, because you may need their help and priority support in the future. American Express or Hertz or Staples can wait a bit, but I'd pay my local printer, designer, web expert, and bookkeeper right on time (and many of them *will* quote *you* net 30 days or even better from your point of view).

Just like you, these are small businesses dependent on cash flow, and you are dependent on them even though you will probably be far from their largest customer. Try to pay them on time.

One final reminder: Bartering is dangerous. Others tend to place bartered services at the bottom of their priority list; there is seldom a completely equitable exchange, the value of the services are often inflated, and any kind of disagreement or falling out will mean that one party or both will be unfulfilled.

It seems easy, but bartering doesn't work well at all, and you'll find that the free health club membership is costing you a valuable day a week in your consulting for that health club owner.

Finally, bartered services are fully taxable (in the United States) under Internal Revenue Service rules, and failure to record them and pay taxes on their fair value is illegal. (Service you *donate* to others, by the way, as to a charity or arts group, are never deductible.)

CYBERSPACE NAVIGATION

There are entire books available for creating advanced web-based marketing (including mine, with Chad Barr, *Million Dollar Web Presence*). However, you have to be very judicious about time use and what's reasonable in the first 90 days or you'll be endlessly *preparing* for web influence but never achieving it.

A fundamental consideration is this: Ignore most web experts, SEO pitches, and claims of quick Internet business. That's because in almost all cases your website is a credibility statement, *not a sales tool.* In other words, people will visit to see if you are real and offer true value *once they hear about you elsewhere.* Thus, market gravity may pull people to your site, but your site alone is not going to pull people to you.

Second, you must find an excellent and fast web (and blog) developer. The best way to do this is to find someone who has created an impressive site for others and to whom you can be introduced. You don't want a schoolkid willing to work for peanuts, nor do you want a large operation that will cost a great deal and, worse, put you at the bottom of its priority list.

Web developers are notoriously late. Here are some guidelines in your search:

- Try to get a personal introduction so that you can get priority treatment.

- Start very simply with just a few pages that can go up prior to your business launch or, if your launch is forced on you, within 30 days.

- Your home page is by far the most important; most people don't go beyond it.

- Don't use links sending people elsewhere. Keep people on your site as if it's a cul de sac.

- Use professionally shot photos and professionally created graphics. Just as in person, you get the opportunity to make only one first impression.

Should you decide to proceed with a blog, create a bank of articles and items to use at various times so you're never under pressure. Plan to blog at least three times per week and never have a site or blog that says "under construction," which screams "new and broke."

We've covered the details of home page real estate and related issues. Before we leave the subject, let's look at the rest of cyberspace as a solid destination or lost space.

You can spend entire days on the Internet, searching for good ideas, reading up on your area of expertise, hunting down contacts, playing games, upgrading software, keeping in touch with friends and family, updating others on your status at the moment, analyzing financial results, pursuing resources ... You will be trying to navigate infinity.

My suggestion is to limit—*formally limit*—your Internet time to fixed, scheduled intervals during your first 90 days. That may seem like heresy, but remember that there are more Internet marketing coaches and social media marketing experts than there are successful professional service firm launches (I kid you not). Don't listen to the noise or get lost in the herd.

What you do on your own (recreational) time in the evening or on weekends is your business. But during your natural work time, use your calendar to schedule when you will search for what. In addition:

- Don't simply accept every upgrade offered and don't search out upgrades unless you're experiencing difficulties with your current versions.

- Don't accept e-mail at any time and don't immediately answer the e-mail you receive. Almost *all* mail marked priority isn't.

- Don't allow Skype or Facebook or YouTube or any other Internet platform to inform you that someone has left a message or has commented on something you've said or done. You can schedule time to check these sources if you must, but don't accept the siren's call to go there when you hear your name whispered in the wind.

- Don't use screen savers (which aren't needed any more in this day and age) of family or personal photos. They are wondrously addictive, and you'll find yourself staring for long periods into what should be a dark screen but instead is an enticing aspect of your past. I know this may sound strange and trivial, but you only have 90 days to get business in the door.

If you waste an hour a day on the Internet doing things you could just as easily do on your down or recreational time, that's five hours a week, about 20 a month, probably about 70 hours during the first three months. Think about that. *That's close to two weeks of solid, productive time frittered away on Twitter or e-mail debates or surfing.*

That means that instead of 90 days to start your success, you actually have about 82 days.

I've been mentioning a lot of don'ts because they seriously undermine newcomer and veteran alike, but have much more of a deleterious impact on the newcomer. But what should you do if you are to successfully navigate your trip in cyberspace?

- Use an e-mail signature with your full, physical address and all other pertinent contact information. You never know when someone will send you a physical copy, a signed contract, or a check.

- In your signature file, state your value proposition, include a testimonial, and anything brief of current interest (e.g., "appearing at the Learning Annex in July"). You should also include your site and blog URLs.

- Use LinkedIn to send messages directly to key people. Unlike e-mail or voice mail, LinkedIn messages are seldom monitored, filtered, or censored by assistants, and will reach the intended recipient personally.

- Don't bother with endorsements on LinkedIn or likes on Facebook or Klout scores, but *do* use contacts on those platforms for written and video endorsements of substance when possible and when they make sense.

- Use Dropbox (or a similar application) or the cloud to immediately sync all your contacts on your desktop, laptop, tablet, and smartphone (or whatever combination you use) so that, no matter where you are, it's simple to find people, return calls, and so forth.

There is no substitute for meeting buyers in the flesh. I received a weekly update this morning from one of my coaching clients, explaining his marketing plans that were met, in place, and being created. But I told him the only metric that really matters is how many buyers you see a week. One of my most successful coaching clients, Colleen Francis, author of several excellent books on the sales process, estimates it may take 29 personal sales calls on a variety of prospects before one sale is made.

You can see that your web work should focus on enabling those contacts to take place, not pretend to be a substitute for them. The small number of people I've been completely unable to help in my coaching of entrepreneurs are those who do not want to pick up the phone or visit people. They tend to hide in cyberspace, as if somehow they'll land and be welcomed on a friendly planet by coincidence.

There are no coincidences in this business. There are only patterns of success and intelligent flight.

THE IDEAL MATE

Anyone who says they have the entire world as their customer will find that they are trying to pursue deer with fishing poles. The deer will run and, even if you were somehow able to corner one, the pole will do no good.

You need to pursue:

- Your ideal customer
- In an ideal manner
- At an ideal time
- In an ideal place
- Under ideal conditions

That may sound almost impossible, but if you make this your goal, you'll come close, and the closer you come, the more likely you are to obtain business. Here's what I mean. You might as well get into the right habits early:

Your Ideal Customer

This is the organization or person who needs your value *or who would most easily recognize and appreciate the value you create for them!* You want to sell computer equipment to the technically savvy and preferably (think of the Market Value Bell Curve) those who are the earliest innovators and adapters.

But you also want to talk to people who are open-minded about discussing needs they didn't realize they had. If you're in the landscaping business, you'd want to meet those who see their homes as a lifestyle investment, not merely a house. The former would be more willing to hear about changes in the plantings, driveway approach, and tree placement than those who merely want a neatly pruned lawn and yard.

Remember that logic makes people think, but emotion makes them act. Hence, no one logically needs a Bentley for transportation or a Bulgari watch to tell the time. But once they emotionally connect to the status of owning such things, they willingly make the purchase, if they have the means (the ideal customer). They may wake up never dreaming they need a second house (or the company needs a new compensation system), but after meeting you they go to sleep feeling they need a second home or at least a thorough review of the compensation system.

Thus, your ideal customer:

- Has need or can be helped to see need easily
- Has means and authority to invest money
- Has or can have an emotional and personal connection for the purchase
- Can act quickly
- Focuses on value and isn't concerned about references, credentials, age, and so forth

Write down six ideal customers, whether you know them now or not:

1. _____

2. _____

3. _____

4. _____

5. _____

6. _____

An Ideal Manner

It's best that clients and customers come to you. No one walks into McDonald's to browse; that buying decision has probably been made before customers even got in the car, but certainly by the time they pull into the lot having spotted the golden arches. Everyone, from retail shops to websites, attempts to draw people to their offerings.

In professional services, that involves market gravity. You may visit prospects, of course, on their turf, but you'd prefer that it be at *their request*. To create this ideal manner, provide as much value as you possibly can in the marketplace so that your name and IP become well known *among your ideal customers*. It doesn't help to be published in *Fortune* magazine if your ideal customers don't read it and aren't impressed by it, but it does help to be published in the *Cleveland Business Weekly* if your closely held, ideal prospects read that.

The ideal manner consists of your ability to meet with people who are eager to meet with you. How might that be arranged for the six ideal customers you listed above?

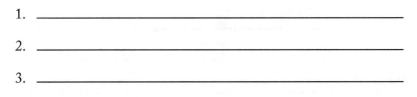

1. _____

2. _____

3. _____

4. _____

5. _____

6. _____

At an Ideal Time

We've established that time is a priority, not a resource, so you have to increase your priority status. But beyond that, there are some times better than others to meet with ideal customers.

For example, in a small, closely held business, if the owner has a spouse or partner, always try to meet with them when they are both available, together. The buyer is often this team, not the formal owner.

For corporations, I always advise an early appointment, not a late one. This usually prevents cancellations and interruptions, and your buyer is always fresher early in the morning. I advise against meeting at meals since they are distracting, not private, and have the potential for undermining the conversation (spilled food, alcohol, colleagues or friends who stop by).

The best time is when a conference room is free with the pretense of getting the buyer away from the phone and distractions (especially in offices with windows); what this also accomplishes *is putting you both on more neutral turf and not in someone else's office.* Find a time of day and a time during the buyer's activities when the discussion will be uninterrupted, fairly intimate, and on neutral ground.

Where and how might that happen for your six prospects?

1. _____

2. _____

3. _____

4. _____

5. _____

6. _____

An Ideal Place

We've already touched on this; people wouldn't buy as many cars without visiting auto showrooms, nor televisions without watching a hundred of them turned on and demonstrated at huge electronics stores.

Yet people often buy insurance in their own homes (surrounded by the environment they want to keep safe and secure), and buy a wide variety of services—from books to vacation spots—sitting at their computers. The ideal place to discuss your value and create a sale is where *the buyer is most comfortable and realizes the benefits immediately.* Time-share salespeople sell their offerings by providing a free lunch and then showing people around the property. Realtors show people homes.

How and where is your buyer most likely to make serious investment decisions? Probably not in the company cafeteria, or during a car ride, or on a plane (I love people who claim they sell to people on airplanes or on elevators—I wouldn't even listen for 20 seconds). They don't want to be disturbed on a vacation or when they're time constrained.

What is the most comfortable place for your six people to make a buying decision?

1. _____

2. _____

3. _____

4. _____

5. _____

6. _____

Under Ideal Conditions

This category may seem to encapsulate those already discussed, but now I'm talking about *you.*

You need to be positive, with high energy and very enthusiastic. You can't be worried about the mortgage, or the leaking washing machine, or your last rejection. You have to have done your homework about the prospect, be well groomed, and have very positive thoughts.

You have the opportunity to make only one first impression, so you can't afford to have put the other criteria into place and then fail because you're down or tired or uncertain about your own value. Use your support system, practice, and listen to comedy or music that elevate your spirits.

Here's a different question: What six methods can you use to ensure you'll be up for you initial calls with a buyer?

1. _____

2. _____

3. _____

4. _____

5. _____

6. _____

You need to approach your market like a laser, not a flying barn. Take the time—an hour, perhaps—to answer the questions listed if you're at all unsure. You can't waste your best time on those who aren't really high-potential clients, and you can't afford your worst efforts on those who really are high-potential clients.

During the second month you should be creating close encounters and meeting with buyers. Ideally, you should have your first sale, no matter how small, which may be to a consumer (individual) or a corporate buyer (organization).

You should be harvesting leads from the work you did in the first 30 days (e.g., calling everyone you know). You should be getting paid for any business you secured during the early part of your launch.

You should have an elementary but professional web presence with credibility for corporate buyers and, if you're very aggressive, products and passive income for consumers if you're also or solely pursuing that marketplace. Your presence on social media, except for pure recreation, should be limited, especially in the corporate market pursuit. You're using technology basically to enhance high touch.

You have recognized clearly who your ideal buyers are on the wholesale and/or consumer dimensions, and you are beginning to infiltrate the streams of influence most effective for them. You can deliver and market simultaneously, and you are justifiably leery about proposed partnerships and alliances.

Now let's turn to your final month, where you should be evolving into a brand name.

THE THIRD
30 DAYS

7

DIVERSIFYING YOUR APPROACHES

There are two primary methods to obtain business: you find it or it finds you. In the latter case, credibility and fees are rarely an issue, so it is the preferred route. It's also easier to fish with a net than a rod and reel in terms of the volume of the catch. We'll examine some approaches that, even this early in the launch of your business, can create huge potential and leverage.

THE MILLION DOLLAR CONSULTING® ACCELERANT CURVE

Those ideal buyers have to be lured *somewhere* and by *something*. So I've developed the Accelerant Curve, as illustrated on the next page.

As you can see, increasing trust and a growing brand drive people from competitive and low-cost (or even free) interactions toward distinctive and very profitable interactions.

The vertical axis is ease of entry (few barriers to learn about you), with high at the top. The horizontal axis reflects increasing revenues *and* decreasing labor intensity as you move from left to right. On the extreme

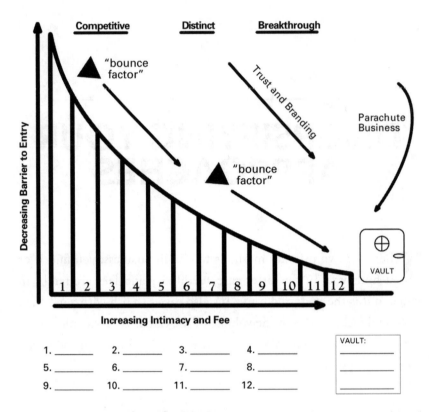

Million Dollar Consulting® Accelerant Curve

right is your vault, containing value only you can provide.* Examples of vault items might include:

- Retainers
- Licensed intellectual property
- Special experiences (e.g., retreats)
- Online membership communities

There are bounce factors along the curve, meaning that certain items of value may propel people forward much more quickly and in larger bounds.

---

* Jerry Garcia once said that it's not enough to be the best, you have to be the only one.

For example, someone reading my $21.95 book *Million Dollar Consulting* might decide to attend my $14,500 Million Dollar Consulting College. When you become very good and very well known, you receive what I call parachute business, with people entering your universe directly on the high-investment right side.

Now here's what I ask you to do. Write down just two items of value that appear for you on the left, in the middle, and on the right. You might choose eBooks or podcasts on the left, organizational audits or coaching in the middle, and strategy work or retainers on the right. Choose just six things that represent you well and can generate interest and business in those separate areas.

Eventually, you'll have 12 or 15 entries across the bottom, and a half-dozen vault items. But for now, create options people can access to involve you in their ongoing needs.

> ### Launch Lesson
> *Don't overload your value on the left of right—too inexpensive or too expensive. You want to lure people in on the left, make money in the middle, and build high margins and long-term business on the right of the Accelerant Curve.*

The importance of using a schematic like this to diversify your offerings and approaches cannot be overstated. It's vital to enable people to easily get to know you, but also vital for them to realize how expensive it can be to do significant business with you.

It's very important to understand that a single intervention—let's take coaching as an example—can be found on the left, in the middle, and on the right. You may do remote coaching by phone and e-mail; significant coaching for middle management that features on-site shadowing and frequent debriefs, and enhanced coaching for executives, where you help them with the media and public appearances.

You're using similar methodology, but with far different impact and therefore value for the client.

After 90 days, you can work more on the Accelerant Curve. For now, try to create just six items of value that can be used to attract, secure, and exploit new business.

Script

Self-script: What two items can I create to make it easy for people to get to know me, what two items will create enough business to pay the bills, and what two items will be seen as uniquely mine of a compelling and unique nature?

TAKING THE ROLE OF EXPERT, NOT CONSULTANT

Right from the outset, start calling yourself an expert.

Experts are people who have an authoritative and comprehensive knowledge in particular areas, *and who have the advisory abilities to transfer that knowledge into pragmatic application for the benefit of others.* The beginning of the definition you'll find in any standard dictionary, but the italics are mine.

Experts disseminate their expertise in a variety of ways, along diverse avenues:

- Speaking
- Consulting
- Training
- Negotiating
- Reporting
- Listening
- Facilitating
- Coaching
- Writing
- Mediating
- Restructuring
- Editing

- Rearranging
- Reviewing
- Prescribing
- Designing

- Counseling
- Diagnosing
- Reacting
- Analyzing

Calling yourself a coach or an editor or a sounding board or a trainer or any other arbitrary pigeonhole immediately diminishes your applicability and reduces your potential buyers. During a vast variety of consulting projects, I've concurrently coached senior managers, spoken at company conferences, written manuals, interviewed potential hires, analyzed poor performance, redesigned evaluation systems, listened to employee grievances, and so on.

My value was enhanced by this diversity, and my expertise—improving individual and organizational performance—was applied on multiple aspects of the project. By identifying myself as an expert, I wasn't limited to a narrow rut identifying me as, say, a coach, making it necessary for the client to bring in other people for other issues.

Too many veterans narrow their appeal and limit their careers through arbitrary titles to describe themselves. They're reduced to a business card instead of enlarged to a source of holistic improvement.

We talked earlier about value propositions. Always state yours as "I am an expert in . . ." (Examples: I am an expert in maximizing the quality of family environments. I am an expert in financial security. I am an expert in the acquisition of new business.)

Launch Lesson

People tend to see titles as commodities, as in "Get me a reasonable coach," or "Find a designer who works by the hour." But they tend to see experts as valuable partners, as in "Find an expert on mergers who can help us make sure we safeguard this investment."

Thus, as an expert you can diversify your approaches and not be beholden to a few methodologies or modularities. When I was starting my practice after being fired, I learned two key words: of course. Whenever anyone asked if I could do something, I said, "Of course." I didn't check to see if it fit into my toolkit or was included under my title. I felt if I couldn't do it immediately, I could learn it prior to starting the project.

I believe in and created the 1% Solution: Tools for Change®. It's very simple math: If you improve by 1 percent a day, in 70 days you're twice as good. (If you don't believe me, grab a calculator and hit 1, times .01, 70 times, and you'll arrive at 2.)

What I've just explained may be your 1 percent for today. I'm going to restate it:

> By seeing yourself and presenting yourself as an expert and not as a title, you vastly open up your potential to be pursued for a wide variety of prospect improvement, to which you can simply say, "Of course."

It's difficult enough to attract new business, but when you proactively limit that new business because you've arbitrarily created too fine a filter based on your title or business card, you're going to have a hard time acquiring business in 90 weeks, let alone 90 days.

When you're asked what you do, reply, "I'm an expert in . . ." When you write or speak, blow your own horn with, "As an expert in . . ." You'll see how this will nicely build your personal brand, as well.

The normal sequence of acquiring information and making use of it looks like this:

$$\text{Data} \rightarrow \text{Information} \rightarrow \text{Knowledge} \rightarrow \text{Wisdom}$$

We have data all around us, which must be combined into useful information. The application of the information constitutes knowledge.

And the evaluation of such knowledge and its application in anticipation of the future is wisdom. We used to call such purveyors wise men. Today, they're experts.

Script

As an expert in maximizing the quality and comfort of travel, I recommend that you invest in . . .

BUILDING YOUR NAME AS A BRAND (YES, ALREADY)

People ask me all the time if they can use their name for their company, fearful that it may seem amateurish. I tell them that it seemed to work pretty well for McKinsey and McDonald's and Dell.

We talked earlier about branding, so I want to focus here on your confidence in using your name right from the start, day one.

The name of my firm is Summit Consulting Group, Inc. That's my legal entity. I've never branded it or used it as a promotional brand. I chose it because I didn't think my name was something I should use so early, and I wanted to give the impression of organizational heft, so the *group* made sense to me.

Of course, I am the group.

When I was politely asked about this (not challenged), I would tap dance all over the room, talking about contract resources, alliance partners, and shadows. It became pretty clear that there was no group, and I was trying to pull a fast one.

Later in my career, a buyer on an airplane—this happened to me exactly once in 30 years—who was to become a client, said, "I'll get my people to talk to your people." Without blinking, I replied, "You're looking at my people." At that point, I had both the confidence and experience to tell me that the buyer didn't care whether I had staff or not, and my value was the selling point, not my payroll.

I tell you this so you can avoid the same mistake. If numbers of bodies were the operating factor behind value, clients would hire the postal service or the 101st Airborne to solve their problems, and that's not something that's ever going to happen.*

> ### Launch Lesson
> *You want your name on people's lips. The best route is usually to shout it in their ears.*

Using your name repeatedly creates your own version of brand equity—that is, there is worth in your name alone, and people will say, "Get me Larry Johnson." (You just don't want them to say, "Get me a *young* Larry Johnson"!) We talked earlier about your entering the streams that influence buyers. This is how you create your own stream.

Here are some alternatives to improve the branding of your name. You may find some obvious, some obscure, and some odious. You don't have to use them all, but you need to give it some thought if you want to land business early and become a known quantity:

- Make sure your name is easy to pronounce. A woman may want to use her maiden name or middle name. A man might want to use his middle name or a shorter version of his name. I met a woman once whose name was something like Rebecca

---

* Lest you believe that McKinsey (or Bain, or BCG, or KPMG, or any large firm) is hired because of the numbers it can bring to bear, let me disabuse you of the notion. They have powerful brands that make them defensible if the board asks why so much money is being spent. It's often an incestuous situation because people leave those firms to join the clients as executives, then bring the firm back in.

Young Teskalefbre. I suggested she simply use Rebecca Young. She liked the idea, but then told me her husband, who was a car mechanic, wouldn't allow it. If this is occupation and not avocation, you had better be your own boss.

- Use your name when you're introduced. Make sure your introducer has it correct at formal events (my notes to the introducer stipulate that *Weiss* rhymes with *ice*, or they'll be likely to pronounce it *Weese*).

- Place your name on your publishing. Don't post on your blog, "Ten Tips for Better Referrals." Instead, call it, "Ann Taylor's Ten Tips for Better Referrals." These things often get reprinted and copied, and besides your copyright, you want your name to be prominently displayed in the title.

- Use the third person. If you're writing a press release or citing your experience or providing content for someone, don't say "Here's what I found" or "My conclusions are ..." Say "Here's what Joan Simmons found" or "William Simpson's conclusions are . . ."

- Put your name on methodology and models, constructs and illustrations. Call it the "Maureen Gladstone Business Audit," or the "John Martin Valuation Visual."

If you do this from the launch of your business, you'll be building that much more momentum for your name to become known and *become valuable in and of itself.* (Tom Clancy and other authors often put their names on books they didn't write themselves; such is the brand power of their names. Your first sale can do this the same way *The Hunt for Red October* did it for Clancy.)

A final aspect of your name and its brand power: in advertising, they talk about repetition. It's not the power of the ad alone, it's the constant exposure to the targeted audience. In your case, as well, you have to repeatedly put your name in front of your ideal buyers—with newsletters, blog posts, op-ed pieces, letters to the editor, articles, interviews, and so forth. It's not just establishing your name, it's keeping it current with your best prospects.

If you do have a tough name but are in love with it—or are married to a similar auto mechanic—at least take solace here: One of the most successful basketball coaches in history is Mike Krzyzewski (pronounced *sha-shev-ski*). I had to look it up to spell it, although I could remember the pronunciation. You can get away with that when you're moving in on a thousand wins.

Script

Hello, I'm Alan (pause) Weiss (pause), and I'm happy to be with you today on this teleconference.

BROADCASTING THE ARRAY OF YOUR SERVICES

By now—theoretically, as I advised in the introduction to read this entire book through before you begin—you're at about the beginning of your third month of your launch. You should have:

- Collected and contacted all possible names of recommenders, prospects, and interested others

- Created basic banking, insurance, legal, and office support—including equipment and logistics (e.g., privacy)

- Created your value proposition (how others benefit) and brands (how to recognize you), with an emphasis on your name

- Begun calling everyone you know and have been referred to

- Begun obtaining appointments and meeting with people

- Begun attracting others, as well as reaching out to them

- Closed your first sale, no matter how small—whether a speech, coaching assignment, consulting project, training, delivery, and so forth

- Invoiced and perhaps been paid

- Begun using technology simply and for your best interests, not within the herd mentality of social media (there's a reason they're not called business media)

- Learned and begun pursuing your most ideal prospects and entering the streams of influence that affect them

- Considered whether your thrust is wholesale, retail, or a combination thereof

You may be slightly behind or slightly ahead. If the former, let's put on more of a push. If the latter, let's exploit early successes.

We've defined *expert* as the ability to disseminate your value in a variety of diverse areas, using a farrago of approaches and avenues. You now need to broadcast that array, since you never know where your future business may originate.

Case Study

I met a midlevel manager at Dun & Bradstreet very early in my practice. We were introduced by a woman who had read an article I had distributed to my list via a hard-copy mailing.

We hit it off well, but he had no real power to hire me, and I wasn't able to convince him to introduce me elsewhere, since he was thinking of leaving himself. Unfortunately, he did, and I lost track of him.

A year later, a woman who heard one of my speeches asked if I could conduct some training for her employer, State Street Bank. She needed the approval of her boss, so I went to Quincy, MA, to meet him—the same man from Dun & Bradstreet. He was happy to see me, and I gave him the full version of what I was doing. He told me that the training project was too low level, and that he'd like to have me consider a project that his boss, the executive vice president, and the CEO, could approve. They didn't want a massive consulting firm, just a "stiletto" approach, and I was "perfect."

I was approved by all over the next month, and walked out with a $350,000 project, one of the largest single projects of my career.

My point to you is this: I was *lucky.* If I had kept his name and broadcast my services constantly, he would have brought me in sooner. Thank goodness his previous interviews went badly for the project. And his subordinate had invited me in for a completely different reason.

I hope you can see the efficacy of seeing yourself as an expert who can operate in a 360° manner—think of it as land, sea, and air. My former contact had become a buyer and/or recommender to major buyers. He chose *not* to buy my training help—although I could provide it—but instead *recommend* me for major consulting help. I, in turn, had to apprise him—in person and by happenstance—of my value beyond what we had originally discussed at his prior job.

If I—and you—had done this more proactively with more contacts, I just might have accelerated my business growth still more. I'm trying to help you avoid my error, not depend on my luck, yet still emulate my good fortune.

So, what can we learn here, even quite early in your practice?

1. Expand the avenues down which you can proceed as dramatically as you can. There's no reason a consultant can't also coach people. Remember my "of course" response. I can learn how to design a program if I have to, and you can learn to work with groups and not just individuals

2. Keep track of nearly *everyone*. It's easier than ever with today's technology, except for one factor that hasn't changed in the last hundred years: discipline. You can't get to it later. You have to have a system and the time to input and update your database of names, the gold in your Fort Knox.

3. Keep in touch with everyone. Find excuses to send even brief items of value. Place them on newsletter lists. Send out press releases. (See my Monday Morning Memo as an example of a brief, weekly way to do this: http://www.contrarianconsulting .com/category/alans-monday-morning-memo.) In this way you both keep your name in front of people and update and cleanse your lists. An old list that's not been used for six months is probably 20 percent inaccurate at that point.

4. As you hear from prospects and learn you craft, keep adding avenues and services that support new and growing needs among you ideal clients. If you're not growing, you're stagnating.

Script
You may not have heard, so I wanted you to know that I've embarked on a dramatic new intervention with clients to ensure the implementation of strategy. Strategy formulation always seems so perfect in three-ring binders or electronic files, but I've been assisting with the real challenges of making it work.

GOING VIRAL

From the dictionary application on my Mac computer:

noun

an image, video, advertisement, etc., that is circulated rapidly on the Internet: *the rise of virals in online marketing.*

Derivatives

virally, *adverb*

> word trends: Most people are now happy to spread viral infections to their friends, family, and work colleagues. They do so not by sneezing on them but by forwarding e-mails, images, or videos that have amused or intrigued them. The influence of this word-of-mouth publicity on brand awareness and sales is enormous, and one of the most common compounds of viral is *viral marketing.* There are now entire companies, known as *viral agencies*, devoted to creating potential *viral hits* for businesses. See also meme.

Origin: 1970s, from Greek *mimēma*, *"that which is imitated,"* on the pattern of *gene*

> word trends: When the British scientist Richard Dawkins coined the word **meme** in his 1976 book *The Selfish Gene*, he wanted a word like **gene** that conveyed the way in which ideas and behavior spread within society by nongenetic means. Since then, the word has been picked up to describe a piece of information spread by e-mail or via blogs and social networking sites. A **meme** can be almost anything—a joke, a video clip, a cartoon, a news story—and can also evolve as it spreads, with users editing the content or adding comments. Common collocates in the Oxford English Corpus are *spread, pass,* and *transmit*: as with the Internet sense of **viral, meme** uses the metaphor of disease and infection.

In many ways, St. Paul was the first viral marketer. He traveled to cities and sent more letters to groups than any other disciple or apostle, and it's his letters today that provide the most vivid pictures of religious activity at the time. His meetings and missives instructed others to go forth in the same manner, thus initiating a viral movement to convert people to what would come to be known as Christianity.

Technology is simply our most recent viral lubricant.

Note in the definitions that we're talking about nongenetic ways in which information is spread, ideas are shared, *and converts are created.*

Apple is an example of a company that has done this magnificently well, with apps that attract people, who talk about them to other people, who require still new apps for their interests. When I bought my first iPhone, there were about 65,000 apps, and today there are over a million. By the time some of you read this first edition, there will probably be nearly two million. Go to an Apple Store and you can use an iPad or experiment with a computer. The Genius Bar will provide direct help for customers. There are Internet sites that relay gossip and speculate on new products, which influences buying trends.

Apple created consumer evangelism.

Launch Lesson

Stimulate people talking about you and your results. Do this with provocation, contrarianism, assistance, and offers they can't refuse.

You can't afford the ancient sales approach of feet on the street, which stands for knocking on every door in the manner of the old Fuller Brush salesmen. You can't afford to hold Tupperware parties, because no one has the time and you don't have a product to test.

Instead of feet on the street, you need a hot spot, not unlike the Internet connection for other devices that can be created on a single iPhone. That is, you need to be someone others want to be around or hear from because you are an object of interest (OOI) who is known to stimulate others.

How do you do this in the first 90 days? Counterintuitively, *you take advantage of being the new kid on the block.* You aren't known, therefore not predictable, not hackneyed—unless you allow yourself to simply follow the tire ruts of slow-moving cross-country skiers. You need, instead, to be a rather fearless downhill skier, creating both speed and enjoyment.

- Present new ideas around your expertise without worrying about their acceptance by the herd. Example: Photographers shouldn't talk about *pictures* but about *memories.* You shouldn't talk about *goals* but about *issues resolution.*

- Position yourself ahead of the curve, not on it. Example: Create a meme about post-heroic leadership or market-led enterprise.

- Hang out with people who matter *in the viral world.* They may not be buyers or recommenders; they are bloggers, reporters, programming chairs, chapter presidents, podcasters, and so forth. They need dynamic, new content. Provide it.

If you do this well, people will come to you and want to give you money.

Script

Your column has been focusing on the dangers of volatility. Why not interview me on the power of volatility, which is not about to go away, and the Volatility Vault I've developed, which enables people to do better in times of great uncertainty?

8

CREATING PASSIVE INCOME

The stereotypical phrase for this is to make money while you sleep. But it's really more like making money 24 hours a day, every week. Think about making a modest $500 a day, *every day*, just by waking up. That's about $180,000 a year. And you can do this right from the outset if you so desire.

Here's how to use intellectual property and technology to create the kind of passive income that conventional wisdom tells you that you must wait for until you have a brand. Use passive income to *create* your brand.

WEB-BASED PRODUCTS AND SERVICES

The World Wide Web is the greatest repository of distinctive and targeted products and services in the history of human interaction. Even those of us born before its advent now take it for granted, but we need to understand the power and performance at our disposal.

Once upon a time, a collector of Norwegian stamps who lived in New Zealand (for example) would have to send letters to dealers and sources to continue his collection. That would include everything from the stamps themselves to albums and supplies. Today, that collector simply visits the web and finds 2,930,000 entries under the search term Norwegian stamps (obviously, as of this writing—it will change tomorrow).

The collector can exchange information, sell stamps (on eBay and elsewhere), buy stamps, trade stamps, verify historical issues, and so on.

If you're a left-handed fly fisherman (or woman; I've never known how to de-gender that), you can find specific gear on the web (71,900,000 results in 30 seconds).

We *know* this is possible, but we don't *appreciate* it as we should. In your first 90 days, you're not going to populate your website with dozens of hardcover books or audio albums for sale. *But you can begin with items of value that will provide some income and, more important, draw attention to you.*

Assuming some preparation time before launch, or a great deal of energy with a sudden launch, here are some ideas for creating passive income and commensurate recognition on your website.

First, use a shopping cart of some kind. Here's an example of one that I've used for quite some time: http://www.1shoppingcart.com. Or you can use PayPal (https://www.paypal.com/home). If you have a relationship with a bank—which you should have; see Chapter 1—you can set up a MasterCard/Visa/Discover merchant account, and you can then call American Express to add them to it (they serve as their own bank).*

> **Launch Lesson**
> *If you find passive income attractive—and I can't fathom why you wouldn't—make it easy for the customer to purchase products. The key to that is automation, which also decreases your own labor intensity.*

Once you have the means to be paid in place, you can offer products and services that look like this:

- Brief podcasts—five-to-eight minutes—on topics around your expertise. For example, if you're a realtor, how to maximize a

---

* I don't want to go into too much detail, but you can have orders automatically billed and credited to your accounts, or process them on terminals yourself, including virtual terminals on your computers, iPad, and/or iPhone—it's that simple.

home's sale price. If you're a landscape architect, how to create pest-free outdoor environments. If you're a business coach, how to gain an hour of free time daily.

Case Study

An attorney I coached decided to make use of these approaches and placed simple forms on his website that could be downloaded for various modest fees. They covered small-business needs for hiring, termination, confidentiality, performance evaluations, and so on.

They were so popular that we created an annual membership (at the time, $6,000) to download as many forms as needed over a year, since he was always adding and updating documents.

This was so popular that he gave up his client practice altogether and made his living from the membership on the web, which he continues to do quite lucratively today.

- E-books of 10 to 20 pages with specific how-to advice. These should have visuals, graphics, and/or photos and are usually best received with checklists and guidelines. Here's an excerpt from my *101 Questions for Any Sales Situation You'll Ever Face*:

    1. Qualifying the Prospect

    This is the process of determining whether the inquiry is appropriate for your business in terms of size, relevance, seriousness, and related factors. In other words, you don't want to pursue a lead which can't result in legitimate—and worthwhile—business.

    Questions:
    1. Why do you think we might be a good match?
    2. Is there budget allocated for this project?
    3. How important is this need (on a scale of 1–10)?
    4. What is your timing to accomplish this?
    5. Who, if anyone, is demanding that this be accomplished?

6. How soon are you willing to begin?
7. Have you made a commitment to proceed, or are you still analyzing?
8. What are your key decision criteria in choosing a resource?
9. Have you tried this before (will this be a continuing endeavor)?
10. Is your organization seeking formal proposals for this work?

Key Point: You want to determine whether the potential work is large enough for your involvement, relevant to your expertise, and near enough on the horizon to merit rapid responsiveness.

- Mini-manuals and documents that serve to improve business flow or personal issues. The case study earlier in this chapter was one such example.

These three quick alternatives can be prepared without a lot of work, used as free marketing devices in the right situation, and serve to create some income and attention on a round-the-clock basis. Price them reasonably—between $10 and $25.

SUBSCRIPTION SERVICES

There are a few forms of periodic subscriptions you can offer: print, video, and audio. You can also offer access, which means that for a given fee, a subscriber has access to a special site or web pages not available to the general public.

While this may seem difficult to accomplish for someone in the first three months, I'll try to make it easy so that the more adventurous among you will be able to pursue additional passive income in these domains.

Print

Print can mean electronic or hard copy. The most pragmatic means here is a newsletter.

There's a school of thought that will tell you there are too many newsletters. Don't attend that school. The reason there are so many is because people read them. The reason is our point in the prior section: high quality, focused content available through the web. Competition *opens* markets; it doesn't narrow them. (This is why Wendy's builds stores across the street from McDonald's—they know people are showing up there to buy burgers.)

If you decide on a weekly edition, use a quick hit (Alan's Monday Morning Memo is a single paragraph); a monthly or quarterly can be longer. I suggest you consider a monthly electronic newsletter. The deadlines are reasonable, you can make it about a page (a computer screen) with three or four key issues, and you can bank them.

By banking them, I mean write four or more in advance and withdraw them from the bank on the deadline. You can always change something at the last minute. You can actually begin these prior to your launch if you have the time. You might acquire only a few subscribers at the outset, but keep the price inexpensive—$150 for a year, for example—and the list will grow. People believe they get what they pay for so, ironically, a price is often more of an allure than getting something for free.

Focus on a few issues around your intellectual property and value proposition that will be of immediate use to your ideal buyers. By including diverse points, you have a better chance of making sure there's something hot for most people (rather than one longer article).

Launch Lesson

Make sure you always send newsletters out on the same day without fail, number your issues, and copyright them. Archive them on your website and/or blog. Use soft promotion to include your services in each issue.

Use a LISTSERV (e.g., databack.com) to automatically handle subscribers, changes, and so on, as well as sending your newsletter out overnight on the web. The charge is very small, and your labor is greatly reduced. I'd advise *not* trying to manage this with your own software.

Video

Video is the most influential medium on the web because it makes the most use of the its potential. However, it needn't be an HBO production.

Informal, brief videos are the key. You can shoot these with your computer camera or a better camera easily purchased on the web (try Logitech, for example, and Snowball is a very good microphone that plugs into USB ports). Choose your background carefully, dress well, and practice (don't memorize) what you want to say. *Keep these to about five minutes.*

You can bank these as well. You can establish a link, a private YouTube site (not open to the public), or circulate them on a service such as Hightail, which can handle large files, for your subscribers. Feel free to use props, and don't be merely a talking head. Minor flubs and errors are fine; these are meant to be personal communications, not polished productions. You may want to have a professional put a 30-second title screen with generic music on the videos, or simply start them by greeting your audience.

As with print, choose topics of immediate import. I'd suggest one topic per video. Again, keep the charges reasonable ($100 is only $2 a week). Charge for an entire year, and send new subscribers all the prior editions, so that you don't have to track hundreds of different renewal dates—everyone renews at the same time.* You can visit my site and see samples of my subscription series, Alan Weiss's Common Sense World View: http://www.summitconsulting.com/seminars/Alans-Common-Sense-World-View.php.

Audio

Your audio subscription should be for podcasts, similar to your videos—short, sweet, and to the point. It's too cumbersome at this point—and you'd need more lead time—for longer teleconferences.

You can record these using software such as GarageBand with a good microphone (see earlier suggestions). You'll have access to generic music,

---

* By the way, all of my offerings are "no refunds for any reason." That will save you a lot of headaches.

sound effects, and so on. If you prepare notes, you can usually record a fine, five-minute podcast with a total expenditure of about 30 minutes.

You can do these in advance, and the advantage is that people listen to them in their cars, on their iPhones, and so forth. Follow the same format you would for video.

Access

One form of subscription is represented by the case study about the lawyer earlier in this chapter. People don't have to subscribe to a periodic mailing or link; they can subscribe to a site.

You can arrange your expertise so that it can be downloaded (as above, in text, audio, and/or video). Let's say you're an expert on plant and facilities power, energy, and conservation. You might include:

- A set of calculations to determine energy efficiency of a plant
- A video on how to conduct an energy conservation audit
- Several podcasts on how to bargain and negotiate with local utilities
- Brief position papers on how to anticipate Occupational Health and Safety Administration (OSHA) visits and prepare for them
- Frequent updates on changes in laws that apply to power generation

The more time you have to plan prelaunch, the more passive subscription income you can implement. But even if day one on your own is launch date, you can create one or two of these to be functioning in the first 90 days.

Script

I've created a special, informal video series on superb organizing skills, which costs less than $2 per week yet will save you tens of thousands a year in reclaiming wasted time.

HARD-COPY VALUE IN A DIGITAL WORLD

There was a time when I made sure my wife or I went to our post office box every day, because my business correspondence, bills, and, most important, checks arrived there regularly. If we were both traveling, I'd pay someone to pick up the mail for us and let me know what had arrived.

Today, we may go there twice a week because we're in the neighborhood or we have a package that demands attention by a postal clerk. Everything else is electronic.

There was a time when an electronic communication was so novel and infrequent that it gained my immediate attention and very careful response.

Today, I have massive filters on my e-mail, rapidly unsubscribe to what I consider irrelevant junk, and simply delete much of the incoming, irrelevant communications.

I won't continue this as one of those derivative and dumb fable stories, but I will suggest that we're seeing the inevitable pendulum doing what pendulums inevitably do—swing back whence they came.

Today, you can gain attention through hard copy because it stands out amid the electronic chatter and there is so much less of it. If you eliminate third-class advertising mailings, the first-class mail is very lonesome, and the primary reason the postal service can make huge cuts and even consider ending Saturday delivery. (If catalogs and circulars were banned from the mail tomorrow, a few clerks in trucks could deliver all the residential mail for a midsized city in a day.)

In terms of passive income, you may want to consider a hard-copy newsletter or flash drive that arrives in the mail, or manuals, or anything else that might make sense out of the electronic mainstream. I say *consider* because this is clearly not a major endeavor, but it is one that might just set you apart.

Newsletter

Try something simple, one to four pages, with several different ideas or content (nothing different from an electronic newsletter). You can create a template on your computer using your word-processing software and have a local printer run them off once a month using the template. Use a four-color layout, include photos and graphics, and have your own editorial. These take advance planning, and you can even subcontract some of the writing. But a newsletter is different and can gain you some visibility outside of the crowd.

Flash Drive

I've noticed that my vehicles now include a port for a flash drive to be used on the entertainment system. These can also be plugged into laptops, irrespective of a local Wi-Fi connection. Hence, they can be appropriate for people traveling. They are inexpensive and can be mailed easily. Why not provide a monthly audio, textual material, or combinations thereof to subscribers? It may sound a bit odd, but it will also be very distinctive.

Manuals

People love lists. I've coached consultants who specialize in image and etiquette, for example, who sell lists and guidelines on how to match colors, appropriate clothing for various events, how to use silverware at a formal dinner, how to prepare certain foods, and so forth. I've helped engineers provide checklists for everything from safety to design procedures. A hard-copy list or manual on plastic or touch paper that can be placed under glass on a desktop, or kept in a briefcase, or even folded in a pocket can have great appeal.

These are just some random ideas, and I wanted to show some creativity. The more mainstream options are the obvious: Books are the ultimate hard-copy product, and despite iPads, Kindle, Nook, and all other electronic means, they continue to sell. In your case, you might consider:

Booklets

You won't have the time to write a 300-page book, but you will have the time to write a 30-page booklet, which—after graphics, front and back matter, and proper layout—will require only about 20 pages of text. I sell five on my site for $7, which you can also buy on Amazon.com.*

- Choose a topic, such as Seven Secrets to Maximize the Sales Appeal of Your Home.

- Write about four pages on each point.

- Include one graphic or photo with each point.

- Create a one-page introduction.

- Create a table of contents.

- Provide a brief author biography at the end.

- Provide *all* your contact information at the end.

- Assign an ISBN number and price.†

- Have a local designer or art student design the cover for you.

You can create a booklet like this easily within a week. Whether you choose to do it in the first 90 days is up to you. Mine are still selling 20 years later.

Script
I'm providing a hard-copy newsletter, not because I don't believe in modern electronic communication, but because I do believe in standing out in a crowd and affording you the opportunity to gain some value in a private and focused setting of your choice.

---

* The Amazon Advantage program allows for self-published works to be sold on the Amazon site.
† International Standard Book Number, required by Amazon and bookstores (along with a bar code). See Bowker at https://www.myidentifiers.com/isbn/main

REMOTE COACHING

In the first 90 days, you can create instant income through remote coaching. I include this in passive income because, even though you're actively engaged, you're home with your feet up on the desk when you do this.*

Your alternatives for remote coaching are the obvious ones: phone, e-mail, Skype. You may also find that more exotic software such as virtual meetings can make sense, though I've always found it to be overkill when I'm working one-on-one.

Remember that I've emphasized that you're an expert, and that your expertise can be manifest in a variety of modalities along a diversity of avenues. One such option is coaching in which you confine the relationship to these alternatives. As a result, you can effectively time shift your work, coaching people down the block or around the world. I Skype weekly with people in Melbourne, Sydney, Perth, London, Birmingham, Regina, and other venues. My 5 p.m. may be their 8 a.m. or vice versa, but we make it work.

Let me show you just how viable and immediate this can be.

First, write down someone who has come to you for help of a professional or personal nature whom you've successfully assisted:

_____

_____

Second, write the nature of the issue, problem, or challenge:

_____

_____

Third, write what you did to help them (e.g., offer advice, solve a problem, provide a skill, alter a behavior, and so forth):

_____

_____

---

* FYI: I consider anything I do within an hour of my home passive income because I sleep in my own bed, have dinner with my wife, and expend very little effort. Many of my development experiences were conducted in my home, a commute that seldom involved traffic.

Finally, record how they improved or why you were successful:

_____

_____

Congratulations, you're a coach! You don't need worthless certificates or diplomas from "institutes." Buyers never care about vague and unrecognizable initials or credentials. The fact is, all of us have coached others during our lives as a natural aspect of human interaction and socialization, especially in the workplace.

Since we've established that you are a highly qualified coach, you merely need to formalize the position by making others aware of that aspect of your value offerings. You may want to include it in your conversation, networking, speaking, publishing, website, e-mail signature, blog, and so on. Offer some coaching pro bono to a nonprofit to obtain a reference or testimonial.

Many people will approach you for free help once they find you've established your own business. Don't allow yourself to be flattered into free work. Instead, offer your coaching expertise.

Tell people that you're sorry you can't provide free help, since you're a for-profit business and have to pay the mortgage, but that you do have reasonable and immediate opportunities to help via remote coaching. (Remote coaching mitigates the concern about expenses for travel on both the client's part and your own.)

Now, here's the key device to bring people on board: Offer options. For example:

> _Gold Program:_ One phone call and two e-mails a week for a month at specified, mutually agreed upon times. Price: $1,500.
>
> _Platinum Program:_ Unlimited e-mails and phone calls over a month, with the agreement that you'll return calls and e-mails within a day. Price: $3,000.
>
> _Diamond Program:_ Unlimited e-mails and phone calls, and a Skype call once a week at a mutually convenient time. Price: $5,000.

You can extend the period from one month by giving a break on the pricing, e.g., three months committed to at the outset would be $1,000, $2,000, and $3,500, respectively, per month. In the last case, you now have a $10,500 project over 90 days. Three of those would give you a six-figure annual income.

Options always increase the choice of a yes by changing the conversation from "Should I?" to "*How* should I?" And you can call the programs by any variety of names. In this example, you could use Advisory, Collegial, and Partnership, if you so chose.

My strong recommendation is that you see yourself as a coach, encourage others to see you that way, and engage in the kind of promotion that brings this to everyone's attention. Coaching, no matter how remote, can often turn into substantial on-site business.

Let's move now to how passive income can contribute to your life balance and health in an otherwise demanding solo practice.

Script

Unfortunately, I can't provide free help or I'd be doing this 100 hours a week and not feeding my family. I hope you can understand my position. However, I do offer quite reasonable remote coaching options that should provide the quality help you need at a very reasonable investment, and we could start immediately.

CLOSE TO HOME: LIFE BALANCE

How do you take care of your relationships and support system and enjoy not a personal life and professional life but *one* life? There are advantages of entrepreneurship that too many don't pursue. I want to make sure you integrate them into your life and work.

DRAWING PEOPLE TO YOU

We discussed earlier the concept of market gravity, and how to attract people in order to lower costs of acquisition, vitiate demands for credentials, and make fee concerns largely irrelevant. We'll expand upon that strategy here in talking about life balance, because real wealth is discretionary time and money is only fuel. (See the figure on the following page.)

You draw people to you by becoming what I call an object of interest (OOI). Above and beyond the tactical and highly pragmatic techniques in the market gravity chart, this is an aspect of your name being the brand and your personal being the draw.

Motivational guru Tony Robbins routinely draws people to his private island near Fiji at about $50,000 apiece (last time I checked) without much of an agenda or support material. People are confident that just being around him will be exciting and help them to grow. My friend Randy Gage (*Risky Is the New Normal*) can draw a thousand

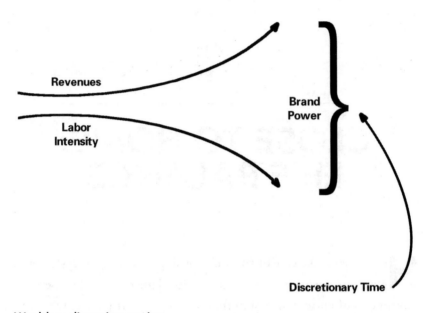

Wealth as discretionary time

people to Thailand to hear him speak because his message of abundance and prosperity is universal and enduring.

People pay $15,000 to $20,000 to be with me for a day in my home or at one of my intimate programs on exotic properties. An author such as James Patterson or Danielle Steel can have thousands of people lined up down the street outside a bookstore for a signing.

You might be thinking: These are examples of people who have made it, with strong brands, huge followings, and well-known names. But we all arrived there through different means in being an OOI. You can, too, and in short order. You're now—sequentially, in this book—almost at the end of the three months. But if you're reading it in advance, as I hope most of you are, you have plenty of time to plan how you spend those three months.

And that's plenty of time to become an OOI. Here's what you should be doing:

- Take contrarian, not merely provocative positions. Point out that the key isn't better sales skills, but to provide the customer with better buying skills. Or make a case that you shouldn't wait for a legal problem to retain a lawyer, or that a casual wardrobe is more important than a business wardrobe.

- Be present in the public square. Write op-ed letters to the newspaper and propose op-ed articles. Speak out at civic and service meetings, with reference to your expertise: "The Soccer Tournament budget needs to be established with what I tell my own clients is a 'contingency mindset,' so that we don't go into debt once again and need fund-raisers to save us."

- Blog and guest blog. Many of us allow others to submit articles for our blogs. Press home a point of view that is irresistible in terms of whetting others' appetites, e.g., "The Pareto principle doesn't work; it's simply an excuse for us not to think about productivity improvement."

- Take leadership roles. Volunteer for your town's committees, for your club's task forces, for charity drives. Be as visible as possible. You'll find yourself elbow-to-elbow with potential recommenders and buyers who are—by dint of your joint efforts for that cause—peers for the moment.

- Contact privately local media personalities. Approach newspaper reporters, talk show producers, public television and radio executives, and magazine publishers. Provide ideas for shows and articles and series. Volunteer your involvement. I was featured on the CNN channel once using this approach, and the technical crew and interviewer came to my house for the shoot.

The key mental set for these types of initiatives is that almost anything *can* be accomplished in the first 90 days. We're not talking about building a bridge, running laboratory experiments, or growing crops. We're talking about launching a professional services firm of one person—you—and you can move to these positions immediately if you have the techniques (herein) and the discipline (within you).

I've found strangers at parties to be instantly interesting, and have sometimes sat next to someone on a plane or train who turned out to be absolutely fascinating. There was no buildup required, no second or third meetings. They were interesting people because they had original ideas they articulated with passion and depth. They stimulated my own thinking and prompted me to want to maximize what time I had with them.

You can play the same role, right from day one.

You need to have the self-beliefs, ideas, and enthusiasm to compel others to want to hear more. You should be able to do that right now.

Script

I'm pleased to be leading the effort to increase volunteers here at the theater, and I want to suggest that we should abandon our focus on young people in these roles and look for senior citizens. They are happy to have a connection with this theater, are serious and courteous, and can be paid with free access to our productions. I'd like to start this immediately.

MAXIMIZING VACATIONS

Since wealth is discretionary time, it's important to know what to do with our wealth. If you use discretionary time working—which is the very definition of a workaholic, using all available time on the job—then I'm not sure I'd admire your choices. Your support system, which we talked about in the first chapter—whether family, friends, colleagues, or others—deserve some reciprocity.

> **Case Study**
>
> I was teaching an extension program at Boston University for entrepreneurs and their lifestyles. Most recognized the need to be stronger about committing time to themselves and their families.
>
> However, an attorney raised his hand and said, "My entire love and life is my work. I enjoy helping clients. So when I'm working at home until midnight or at the office early, what difference does it make so long as I'm fulfilled? I don't need to play golf or read great books."
>
> "Do you have a family?" I asked.
>
> "Yes, a wife and two children," he replied.
>
> "What about them?" I said.

No matter what your finances, especially in the early going, take a physical calendar that shows an entire year at one glance* and mark off the vacations you intend to take over the next 12 months, be they trips to Europe, weekends at the beach, or day trips. Put those in your calendar and then work everything else around them.

Factory workers in Germany often receive six weeks of vacation these days. German productivity is relatively high. What kind of union do you have? Please don't tell me you can only afford to take a week or an occasional day here and there.

In almost 30 years of running my solo practice, I've had only three conflicts that could not be resolved, and I never sacrificed vacation time for any of them. Usually a client can change his or her date, or you can shift the project in some way. But if you view vacations as low-priority time on the calendar, or something you'll fit in when you can get to it, you'll take very few.

* I believe the best of these are made by Filofax.

Time is not a resource. Time is a priority. Ergo, you have to appreciate and support the great priority of taking time with your family and/or time for yourself. Your batteries need recharging, and you're working to improve your life, not living to improve your work.

There are, moreover, two kinds of vacation time. One is what I've already described. The other is vacation you add on to a business trip. Some people feel these are second-class vacations, but I differ on that. They can be great opportunities.

My wife and I traveled around the world during a project commissioned by State Street Bank, which had offices involved in Sydney, Hong Kong, London, and Luxembourg. I paid for her airfare, of course, but the rooms were paid for by the client, and I had a day's work in areas where we'd stay for several days (and I'd pay for those room nights).

If you live in Boston and have a client in New Jersey, a quick trip to the Jersey Shore in the summer is rather nice, and conversely, a nice trek to the ski slopes of New England make sense in the winter.

> ### Launch Lesson
> *You don't have a personal life and a business life, you have a life. There's nothing wrong with maximizing your personal pleasure and business effectiveness at the same time.*

In the first 90 days, you may not want to take many vacations. But you should be planning for some in the not-too-distant future, and organizing your schedule so that you know when you can and cannot fit future business into your calendar.

My policy while *on* vacation is to stay reasonably abreast of work. In other words, I don't mind stopping work at home at 2 p.m. and hitting the pool if I've accomplished my objectives for the day. Similarly, I don't mind taking a cell-phone call on the beach or checking e-mail twice a day while on vacation. You're not very secure if you feel this is an on/off switch that can be set in only one direction.

Work/life issues are more of a rheostat, where you can control the specific degrees and settings.

Case Study

I'm sitting on the beach in Aruba and checking my office messages. I return the call of one client who didn't realize I was away.

"Hi, John, it's Alan Weiss returning your call."

"What's the sound in the background?"

"Oh, that's the sound of the breakers. I'm about ten yards from the water in Aruba."

"Alan, you're such a kidder."

"Ah, you've caught me again."

My wife will often turn to me on the beach and say, "Did you pay for our vacation yet?" (This is usually on the first day.) Returning phone calls and e-mail takes perhaps an hour out of a long, relaxing day, and I'm happy (and secure enough) to do it. Don't be doctrinaire or inflexible, and live your life flexibly and effectively.

Script

I'm sorry, but I'll be away during that week in July. Could we reschedule to the prior or next week? Or could we use that week to send out the survey forms while I'm away? What works best for you?

UTILIZING YOUR SUPPORT STRUCTURE

Life balance is, ironically, often pursued unilaterally. That's like pushing a car instead of driving it.

There are no ideal percentages or divisions to achieve balance. When people ask me how much family time should be allotted, I say, "About 64.36 percent." Your life isn't a pizza to be sliced into eight servings.

In the first 90 days, you have to learn and practice true balance. That means discipline and scheduling *coupled with* doing some things when the spirit moves you and you're most likely to be successful and effective. There's nothing wrong with picking up the kids at 3 p.m. on Wednesday or taking a swim at 11 a.m. on Friday, just as there's nothing wrong with working on a proposal at 10 a.m. on Saturday or calling a hard-to-reach prospect at 6 p.m. on Monday.

You have a life. You have time. You make choices.

Here is some help with those choices and your support structure:

1. Understand that time is a priority, *not a resource.* This is very hard for some people to appreciate. There are 24 hours in every day. They are allotted according to your determination of need under ideal circumstances.

    Your body may cause you to collapse after a day of no sleep, thereby claiming a priority. But more commonly—consciously or unconsciously—you allocate time based on the priorities in your life. Thus, if you tell me that you don't have time to see your kid's soccer game, you're really saying, "I choose not to allot my time to that, but to finishing this proposal." That may be an intelligent decision, in order to pay for soccer lessons, but recognize that it's a choice based on priorities, not the absence of available time, which you do have.

    The question for you, if you truly see time as a priority and not a resource, is how you want to *deliberately and proactively allocate it.* Too often, it's done for you. In school, you were told where to be and when. In organizational life, the boss told you what to do, and the organization had expectations and rules. But as an entrepreneur, you have the potential to control these priorities.

That's why I can make business calls from the beach or take a weekday afternoon at the pool. I'm not allowing others to determine my priorities. One definition of disempowerment is that state of constantly sacrificing your own objectives in order to allow others to meet theirs—subordinating your priorities for others.

2. Involve significant others in your business condition. I'm not saying all business decisions or even planning, but your spouse, partner, and others close to you should be informed about the nature and circumstances of your business.

    Too often, a spouse is assuming things are much better than they are because he or she has not been told of the cash flow, prospects, rejections, and so forth. The excuse is not to burden others or cause undue worry, but those reasons are specious.

    My formula is to have at minimum a weekly meeting with your significant other* for perhaps 30 minutes. Discuss:

    - Significant victories and defeats and any patterns they suggest
    - Prospects, the pipeline and generation of new business
    - Existing customers and referral business
    - Finances and cash flow
    - Your emotional state

The absolute worst thing you can do is to ignore your support system and try to carry *all* burdens and stress on your shoulders. That's actually

---

* My wife and I debrief at dinner every evening, over a drink. She provides great insights and is always abreast of exactly where my business is. If you have children of an age where they could learn and contribute, include them as well.

selfish and self-defeating. You need a sounding board, sources of new ideas, and validation of your own good work.

Talk to your partner regularly, not when you get around to it.

> ### Launch Lesson
> *You don't need an advisory board so much as you need your loved ones to be on board.*

3. Collegial help. Believe it or not, others have done what you're trying to do!

    Be careful in your choices, but try to find colleagues who a year or so ago were where you are today. They are closest to ground zero, and if you choose wisely, you can get invaluable advice and feedback from these sources.

    I advise *against* professional trade associations in your field because they are often just an excuse for members to gather and lie to each other about how well they're doing. You can network at such events and perhaps cull two or three people with whom you can interact on an ongoing basis.

    You can offer the reciprocity of giving them feedback if you're asked, sending them referrals, or simply buying them dinner. I wouldn't make this overly formal, with scheduled meetings, but rather the occasional meal, Skype call, or e-mail. These people can be extremely helpful with challenges such as:

    - Local financing and credit sources
    - Referrals
    - Evaluation of sales situations and progress
    - Appropriate fees*
    - Local help, such as travel planners, printers, and so on

---

* That is, *if* they believe in value-based fees and don't engage in hourly billing. You don't want to be talking to the latter.

Create your support structure *and then utilize it*. You're a solo entrepreneur, not the Lone Ranger.

> **Script**
> *Let me give you an overview of where I think my best prospects are and how to approach them, and tell me if you agree and how I might obtain their business even more quickly.*

INVESTING WISELY

As money comes in, there are two great temptations:

1. Spend it.
2. Hoard it.

I believe you prepare for success, not failure, so let's operate on the assumption your first 90 days produces solid revenue with clearly more in your pipeline. Here are my recommendations for what to do with it.

- Pay yourself first

  Tithe to yourself. Take 10 percent of *all* business income, exclusive of expense reimbursement, and place it in a separate account. (Change the percentage to suit yourself.) Thus, if you make $3,500, $350 is placed aside. If you are faithful to this regimen, you will have a very nice reserve fund growing.

- Pay your bills*

  Pay your normal living expenses. I suggest you do this twice a month, on the 1st and 15th. That way, no bill will ever be overdue (your credit rating is a huge asset if it's in good shape),

---

* My premise in this book is that you don't cut down to starvation rations but lead a prudent lifestyle at the outset, so you don't buy a new boat either.

you don't spend unnecessary time paying bills daily, and you have a regimen.

Pay local people first. Small businesses are cash-flow dependent, as are you. This will always give you their priority should you need something in a rush.

- Maximize your retirement plans

  Put everything you legally can into tax-deferred plans funded by your company, e.g., SEP-IRA, 401(k), and so forth. Although paid for by after-tax funds, your normal IRA or Roth IRA should also be funded. Make sure you've chosen investment vehicles consistent with your age, risk tolerance, and market conditions.

- Save for fixed large expenses

  This would include a wedding for a child or college tuition (or private- school tuition prior to that), anticipated surgery or medical bills that aren't insured, vacations, and so forth. To this day, if I have an expensive speaker scheduled for one of my programs, I escrow the money immediately, even if the speaker hasn't requested payment until the time of the event.

- Create your slush fund

  This isn't a term used very often today, but it's meant to be an amount of money that is used flexibly for the unexpected. Two examples:
  - You incur an unexpected tax bill and penalty for a prior year due to an error you made at the time. Or your daughter is unexpectedly offered a semester abroad in the next school year that will require funding in addition to tuition.
  - You encounter a marketing experience or potential that you didn't know existed but can't afford to miss. Or you find that your computer system has been infected and must be entirely replaced.

These are issues you generally don't budget for *except* through a slush find.

> **Launch Lesson**
> *You're not well advised to place all money in one big lump and try to determine which vehicle makes the most sense. Create distinctions and choose intelligent investment vehicles for each.*

In addition, I suggest these investing-wisely practices:

- Always try to work with two banks. You never know when one may change its policies, personnel, hours, or locations. Try to establish banking relationships in two places in order to see where you're best received and where the best deals are on credit and investment.

- Put the preponderance of your investments and financial dealings in one of those banks. That may include securities, mortgages, lines of credit, savings accounts, and so on. You want to ideally create enough of a presence to be a trust customer or private banking client (different banks use different names). This relationship usually provides more favorable borrowing rates, access to key officers, waived fees, more flexible online banking, and so on.

- Keep enough money in liquid form so as to be able to draw upon it and use it quickly. Don't place the preponderance of nonretirement assets in CDs that mature in six months or more, for example. Don't speculate with this money. You're a professional services provider, not a day trader.

- Use overdraft protection on your business account. In the event you need to cover a check and don't have funds readily available, the overdraft will automatically kick in and protect you. The small fee for this is far better than the black eye of a returned check or unpaid bill (or lost opportunity).

- Try to stay debt free, except for your mortgage. It's fine to use credit cards as *temporary cash replacements* so long as you repay the cash each month. Too much debt creates too many interest charges and trouble with your credit score. It can also delude you into thinking things are better than they are. (Suggestion: Try leasing your car instead of buying it with a bank loan.)

You will be making money if you follow my earlier advice. Follow this advice, and you'll keep it and/or apply it wisely.

Script

I'm interested in bringing all my business to one bank. What officer might advise me about this and inform me as to the benefits of creating that kind of relationship here?

PROCURING ONGOING HELP

You may need ongoing help to deliver business. Let's think positively. Here are the reasons to subcontract on a continuing basis:

- You need help with the sheer volume of the implementation; for example, interviews or workshops contracted for.

- You need specialized expertise you don't possess and are not interested in learning; for example, financial analysis.

- You will not learn anything new from the activity and can use your time for better things; for example, let someone else interview customers while you find new clients or develop more IP.

- You have legitimate conflicts that you can't avoid, and you can't be in two places at the same time.

- You want to develop backup resources well in advance of any actual needs.

All of these are valid reasons to consider subcontracting. You don't want to desperately search for people with your back against the wall. My experience is that a relatively few people *whom you can trust implicitly* will always trump a cast of thousands who are distant from you and may not share your beliefs and passions.

Try *never* to use a family member as part of your ongoing help. You probably won't get a first-rate job done and will almost certainly engender an eroding relationship. As nearby, simple, and often even economical as this alternative may appear, it's a rat's nest of enduring agony and poor work.

There are legions of people who are extremely adept at delivering but don't like (or hate) to market themselves. They constitute your symbiotic relationships. You can find them at trade and professional meetings (American Society for Training and Development, Society for Human Resource Development, Institute of Management Consultants, National Speakers Association, et al.); among moonlighting professors and academics; even among graduate students who need some work, preferably in their area of expertise. You can even find them among ex-client personnel. (Don't be fooled—not nearly everyone who worked *for* a client can work *with* clients.)

Launch Lesson

Try to find some people early who are high quality, can use the work, and with whom you get along well.

Never allow people you pursue for subcontracting work to read any of my books. Their default position will always be to charge by the hour, and you will be much better off if you accept that primitive, illogical system, which, here, will obviously work in your favor (as opposed to their billing by their value to you).

Ask for a rate but give an assignment with a capped number of hours. For example, suppose you want someone to run five focus groups of 90 minutes each. Build in some preparation and debriefing time (either with you or in written reports) and agree on the number of hours. *Then stipulate in a brief contract that you accept their rate for that capped number of hours, and anything over that they may require in the event will not be compensated.* You need to firmly control the running meter of billable hours (just ask anyone who has ever so much as asked a lawyer the directions to the restrooms and received a bill for a six-minute charge).

In return for these types of agreements, you can commit to giving these people your top priority in terms of future assignments. But keep it on this basis, not pity or sympathy. I've found consultants paying subcontractors $2,500 a day when equally good (or better) people are around for $750. You'll be told that delivery is the most important element of any client engagement, but it's not: business acquisition is. And there are so many people who are poor at business acquisition—the accelerated topic of this book—that they are plentiful in numbers for those seeking delivery help.

In other words, *it's a buyer's market.* So don't ruin your margins by lavishly paying delivery people who are where they are because they can't do what you're doing: providing others with work.

Another area of ongoing help is your business support team: legal, financial, design, printing, technological, and so on. Always have a Plan B. Some people retire early or die young.* Some people's work declines. Some become so successful that they forsake you for larger business (but without telling you). You can't allow that kind of risk to develop.

---

* When I asked the new printer I had chosen if he knew what killed my former printer at age 48, he said, "I'm not sure, but I am sure about one thing: This job can kill you." I've been with him for 25 years.

So create a backup for your key advisory and logistics resources. Your estate, intellectual property, litigation, and contract attorneys may not be in the same firm. Or, if they are, they may not be of equal help. I've just moved my intellectual property work from my estate-planning attorney's office to my litigator's office because the new IP attorney at the former is a shrill, unprofessional woman. Fortunately, I had known that my litigation attorney could do this kind of work, had the resources, and would welcome the additional business at any time.

You're not being disloyal by occasionally using another resource or at least sounding one out and becoming familiar. This is help you'll continually need, and you want to make sure you have ample contingent actions in place.

Speaking of continually needing something, let's turn now to your success beyond the first 90 days.

PART III REVIEW

Fortunately, expertise doesn't require a diploma or lengthy time of study. You can begin to manifest it immediately.

A MORE DETAILED LOOK AT THE ACCELERANT CURVE

I developed the accelerant curve to demonstrate that you can increase fees and the intimacy of client relationships *at the same time that you decrease labor intensity*, a dynamic we've discussed throughout the book. Decreasing labor is almost as important as increasing revenue. If your labor *increases* with increasing revenue proportionally, *you arrive at a point at which you simply can't take on any more work.*

That's a severe and sometimes fatal point in professional services firms' growth, and it is a serious mistake in one's thinking to believe that there is a ceiling of work you can take on. Just as in the advance from subsistence agriculture to abundance agriculture—and using excess crops to trade in the improvement of one's lifestyle—we must generate more revenues than merely those that pay immediate bills. We have to create retirement, education, insurance, and recreational abundance funds.

In other words, we can't be subsistence professionals.

For the purposes of this review, let's focus on just a few of the features of the Million Dollar Consulting® Accelerant Curve:

1. *Movement:* The idea is to move buyers swiftly down the curve after a low barrier to entry allows them to easily find you and learn about you. Hence, free products and services (e.g., booklets,

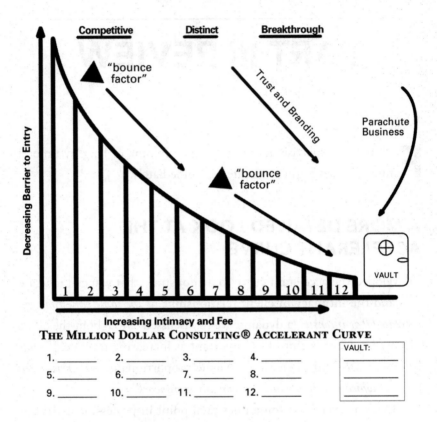

THE MILLION DOLLAR CONSULTING® ACCELERANT CURVE

1. _____   2. _____   3. _____   4. _____

5. _____   6. _____   7. _____   8. _____

9. _____   10. _____   11. _____   12. _____

VAULT:
_____
_____
_____

teleconferences, articles, podcasts) attract people, but also entice them to move toward additional value with moderate fees (e.g., coaching sessions, audits, workshop attendance).

2. *Accelerated movement:* The bounce factors are those offerings that create more velocity down the curve. Buyers don't have to stop and partake of each offering. They may go from a free teleconference to a listing for a home, new lawn services, an insurance trust, an organizational redesign effort, or customer surveys. I've tried to show that this can be a retail (consumer) or wholesale (corporate) application.

3. *Degrees of interaction:* You may have a single methodology— let's say it's coaching—that appears several times on the accelerant curve because it varies in its application. That is, you

have *options*. Toward the left, your coaching may be remote: by phone and e-mail, over the course of a month. In the middle, your coaching may involve weekly Skype calls of an hour and unrestricted phone and e-mail consultation for 60 days. On the right, you may have one or two personal meetings a month and unlimited Skype, phone, and e-mail for 90 days or more. The left may entail solely those conversations, while on the right you also will review tapes of speeches, engage in role plays, and observe meetings. There are significantly different fees for these significantly different interactions. (Note that you can start with right-side coaching immediately upon launching your business if you've been able to prepare and have the right kinds of contacts.)

4. *Moving toward unique:* As you move from left to right, you move from competitive (many people are doing teleconferences on better teamwork); to distinct (relatively few are providing help on differentiating between teams and committees and how to improve each); to unique (you are the only person with an approach called A Team of One, showing how everyone interacts differently every day based on the situations that arise). In your vault are your unique offerings, usually trademarked, that may include licensing, retainers, and other offerings that only you provide based on your repute. Remember that it's seldom good enough in the long term to be "the best." It's better to be "the only one" (Jerry Garcia).

5. *Numbers of offerings:* You don't need dozens of offerings at the outset. You can always build and change the curve offerings. At the outset, I'd recommend that you have or create a half-dozen low-barrier offerings on the left; three or four mid-range offerings; and one or two high-end offerings. Worry about the vault later. In this manner, you've created both the allure and ability to accelerate buyers to the right.

6. *Parachute business:* Finally, be alert for and open to some business that may simply drop in on the right. Don't move it to the left. This may be from people who have known you, referrals, or merely serendipity. If someone is interested in a new strategy for their business's growth, don't suggest that you provide a workshop on planning.

The accelerant curve is very useful to people new to professional services because it allows them to differentiate the value (and fees) of their offerings, taking that sweet spot we discussed early on and expanding its application to a variety of options. Remember that you need to *both* attract people with no perceived obligation on their part *and* provide enticement for them to become more involved with you in relationships of greater intimacy and value *while* decreasing labor intensity.

The greater the trust, the more clients will depend upon you to determine how much labor is required. The less trust, the more they'll demand that you constantly be present.

YOUR EXPERTISE

Your value is as an expert. It's easy to forget or ignore this when you're starting your practice or business. The first sale is to yourself.

How do experts behave? They generally look like this:

- They know a variety of good ways to accomplish results. There is seldom one royal road.

- They aren't afraid to voice opinions and ideas. They don't hold back, waiting to see what the majority says.

- They decide on the route; they don't allow the customer to determine it. (Apple gives options for its computers, but they don't allow customers to demand things—in either design or engineering—that are outside of those permitted options, or they would be out of business.)

- They use a variety of means to deliver their expertise—writing, recording, consulting, speaking, coaching, facilitating, advising, and so forth. They suit their means to the client's needs.

- They're cited by others. That is, they publish through third parties and speak at others' events.

Keeping the accelerant curve in mind, you may publish and speak for free at first, left-side activities that enable people to appreciate your value easily.

The more you focus on clear expertise, the more your activities will support you. Remember, the entire world doesn't constitute your customer. You want the ideal relationships that are supported by clarity in terms of what you provide. Once your expertise is established (I help you close business faster with less cost of acquisition), you can determine the array of such services (consulting with sales forces, coaching sales managers, setting sales strategies, and so on).

Think of building this diversified portfolio of your offerings around the central core of your expertise right from the outset. It's the kind of mentality that builds an exciting and continually growing practice far beyond the first three months.

INCOME WHILE YOU SLEEP

You may want to regard the left side of the accelerant curve as marketing and the right side as business, with the middle being some of both. People love to talk about passive income and making money while they sleep. It's probably too early to spend a lot of time on this in the first 90 days, but steps you take now for other reasons could result in significant alternative income in the future.

First, you have to consider that people pay a lot for high touch (hence, the increasing intimacy as you move to the right on the accelerant curve), but that high tech in today's world enables high touch. E-mail is one dimensional, but GoToMeeting, Virtual Meetings, and Skype are just some of the examples of what I call Dimension 2.5:

Dimension 1: E-mail
Dimension 2: Phone contact
Dimension 2.5: Live contact via technology
Dimension 3: Personal meeting

You can create solid client relationships with minimal or no Dimension 3 involvement. Examples:

- *Retainers:* You are a sounding board and advisor as needed. While not passive in the sense that you're doing nothing, it is minimal and infrequent labor.

- *Licensing:* This is true passive income, in which a client pays you to utilize your intellectual property through the client's auspices without your direct involvement (other than some initial training or occasional support, perhaps).

- *Downloads:* You may provide key legal forms for small businesses, or manuals for consumers, or other downloadable help. Think of the websites you probably access now that provide information for various needs.

- *Hosting:* You can host discussions or even mediate conflicts using web-based tools. Webinars are popular devices to attract people at little or no cost to involve them in your work, as an example.

One of the greatest benefits, however, is that you are instantly global in today's cyberspace world. You should consider IP and offerings that are not culturally bound, but rather pragmatically useful for everyone.

It's never too early to think about passive income, so long as you don't allow it to be a distraction in the first 90 days. Just bear in mind that many of your initial actions can also lend themselves to passive income in the near-term future, certainly within the first year. For example, creating a teleconference is fine short-term marketing. But you may also use a series of these as products for sale farther down the road. So record the first one—don't just do it live and forget about it—with an ear toward it being part of a series. That's what I mean by thinking of passive income based on your near-term business development activities.

Finally, keep the *branding* imperative in mind. Anything you can do to build your brand is a benefit, and products can do that. I once was of the opinion that products and passive income were successful only *after* a brand had been established, but I was dead wrong (and I want you to benefit here from my learning). Just ensure that your products and services are consistent with the brand or brands you intend to promote.

Put your name (or the brand name) on them. That's another example of thinking ahead and leveraging initial marketing activities toward longer-term passive income potential. Too many professionals ask themselves, "Why didn't I originally name this … ?" or "Why didn't I anticipate this could have been a series?" Think of synergies and future potential.

Passive income (products and services) can promote your brand, your brand can promote your passive income, and both can accelerate buyers down the accelerant curve. There's no reason not to be thinking that way right from the outset, leveraging as you go.

THE FULL LIFE

This may be the most important review of them all, because you're not engaging in your business for the sake of the business, which is basically an enabler for you to have a great life.

I grant you that passion for your pursuits is vital, and you may well love your business management, implementation, and involvement.

But the difference between someone who loves their business and a workaholic is a holistic life. The gestalt of your life is the key.

It's easy to be sucked into business details, support, and stress, particularly during the first 90 days. I can even make a case that if there's any time your practice should absorb you, it's during this critical period following launch. However, and perhaps counterintuitively, if you want to achieve a healthy start, you can't totally immerse yourself in your business.

Here are some important considerations that apply during the first 90 days and, of course, thereafter as well:

Perspective

I've tried to provide some metrics in this book to inform you about how well you're doing. But this is often uncharted water. I remember a client bragging to me once that his annual compound growth was 22 percent, unprecedented in his business.

"Great," I said, "but how do you know it shouldn't be 34 percent?"

He simply sat there, stunned for a minute, before asking me how we could investigate whether he was reaching his potential.

You may acquire business your first week, which doesn't mean you don't have to exert yourself anymore. You may not acquire it within 90 days, which doesn't mean you should stop and give up at that point. Each of us is different, as are our businesses and prospects.

Thus, the perspective you need should come from your family, close friends, and trusted colleagues. The only way to gain it is to:

1. Take time away from the business to invest with people who are knowledgeable and empathetic about your intentions.

2. Invest time in listening to them and meeting their needs, since the highest-quality feedback should be based on reciprocity.

You have to give to get. You have to share with others and allow them to share with you to have meaningful exchanges about your progress rather than an offhanded "that's great" or "too bad" when you bring them news. You can't create these dynamics if you're up to your eyeballs in your business every waking minute.

EMOTIONAL SUPPORT

No matter how confident you are, no matter how strong your self-esteem, you are going to have some emotional twists and turns. A prospect will get nasty, you'll receive rejections, a promised contract or payment won't appear, you'll worry about money (even though you may have established a reserve—people always tend to worry about money).

You need someone—preferably immediate family, whether you're married or not, have a partner or not—who can buoy your spirits. When you're depressed—not clinically depressed, but have what we all know as the blues—you have a dampener covering your talent. You can't operate on all cylinders and you simply won't be as effective as you have the potential to be.

When you combine perspective and emotional support, you arrive at people who truly care about you and with whom you feel comfortable sharing your victories, defeats, and *uncertainties.* To this day, my wife and I debrief over dinner every evening. We live in a big house, don't necessarily see each other that much during the day, when she's at board meetings or running errands, and I'm working in my home office or out at the pool.

But in the evening, she'll tell me about her appointments and meetings—reciprocity is important on every level—and I'll tell her about my progress: writing, new business, new ideas, frustrations with scheduling, and so on. Sometimes she gives me ideas, tells me I'm charging too little, or observes that there's nothing much more I can do than grin and bear it. She'll agree when she thinks someone's a jerk, and tell me when I'm being a jerk.

We've been married for 45 years.

I don't insist on a long marriage, or any marriage at all, but I am suggesting that you and I need emotional support on a regular basis, not once a week and not by phone. We need people who can look us in the eye and offer advice who have our best interests in mind, not their own. I know of no chapter, meeting, or professional association where that's going to happen.

Relationships and Money, Money and Relationships

I want to reiterate here that the two issues that are most distracting in small-business launches *and* sustainability are relationships and money.

I've addressed relationships already, with this exception: lousy ones. Whether these are friends or family or colleagues, you need to exorcise unfixable relationships from your life because they will drag behind you like an anchor. One woman I coach has a nephew who is unrelentingly negative—he, himself, doesn't have a job—and tells her that her consulting efforts will never amount to anything. Even after extensive interviews on television, he told her she was lucky. We agreed that she should see him only at two unavoidable holiday events each year, and not speak to him at those. She's far happier, and has since closed major pieces of business. She doesn't know how he feels about that and doesn't care.

You have to relentlessly remove sour relationships. Even if they don't directly impact your business, they will impact your life and distract you from your business. Just as a lousy client creates problems for you with good clients (because of distraction and stress and inappropriate demands), so will a lousy relationship. Some people just don't feel good about themselves (poor self-worth) and their response is to attempt to pull others down to their level through degradation and sarcasm.

Get rid of them or they will be successful and you won't be.

Finally, let's be candid about money, which is not wealth but merely fuel for wealth. Concerns about money can undermine the relationships we've been talking about, which is why I've combined these two vital topics in one segment. Too many otherwise supportive spouses and partners have said once too often, "But what if you don't get any business? How will we pay our bills?"

I've even heard this from two-income couples, where the one raising the questions makes enough to pay all the bills.

Ideally, you want a cash reserve in the bank when you launch your practice. There is no ideal amount; the more you have, the safer you'll feel. Obviously, you'll have more if you plan your launch than if you're forced into it. (For those of you reading this book who are merely contemplating your own business launch, I'd suggest you establish a fund *now*, because your security in any organization is far less than it once was, and that's not about to change any time soon. You can always use the money for something else if you stay where you are.)

I wrote this book so that you can begin to generate income within 90 days or immediately thereafter (having laid the groundwork) so that money (and relationships) aren't as difficult. However, please keep these sources in mind if money is an issue:

- *Savings:* You're saving for something, and this is it! I've seen too many people who regard savings as untouchable, which rather defeats the point.

- *Retirement funds:* This is your money. In best case, if replaced within 60 days, there is no penalty. In worst case, you'll pay tax on it at your current rate, which won't be too bad because you're not generating huge amounts of cash at launch (if you were, you wouldn't need this money). Consult your financial advisor, but bear in mind that these funds, too, are your savings and can be used.

- *Home equity loans:* At this writing these are deductible on taxes (in the United States) and you often need pay back only interest fees each month until you choose to also pay back principal. Your house is an asset and can be used to fund your business.

- *Other loans:* I'm not in favor of credit-card debt because it's expensive and impacts credit ratings. If you can pay the loaned amount back within a month, however, that's fine. These are for short-term use; for example, while waiting for a promised check from a client. But I'd try to keep credit-card balances at zero if at all possible.

- *Family:* I've mentioned the danger of family help when it also becomes business advice. However, you may be the beneficiary of money coming to you from family members that they will advance earlier than anticipated for a good cause and with no strings attached. These aren't loans but are gifts. Don't be embarrassed to pursue them, because they are meant to be of help and support.

I would attempt to maintain a conservative lifestyle, refrain from major purchases (boats, second homes, more vacations), but support what you currently have (school tuitions, existing vacation home, normal entertainment). If you continue to lead your normal life, you'll find that your new venture will begin to fit it like a glove.

In other words, you'll be in good hands.

EPILOGUE: BEYOND THE FIRST 90 DAYS

10

THE VITAL NEED TO BUILD AND NURTURE SELF-ESTEEM

OVERVIEW

How to use early success to create evergreen success and build a personal and extended belief in your own value will now be key. The first sale is to yourself. But what of years of sales that will make you wealthy?

SELF-TALK

I once thought that a lack of capitalization was the major reason that new practice launches failed.

I was dead wrong.

Having coached, counseled, and mentored entrepreneurs for nearly 30 years, I can tell you unequivocally that the major cause of failure is a lack of self-esteem. Short of major therapy, and focusing on the highly pragmatic, the most direct route to enhanced self-worth is positive self-talk.*

---

* The best book on this subject is Martin Seligman's *Learned Optimism* (Vintage, 2006).

The words you use with yourself inform your behavior, and your behavior influences how others think of and react to you.

There's a difference between how good you are at any given endeavor—efficacy—and how good you feel about yourself—esteem. They can be independent variables, as you can see in the chart below.

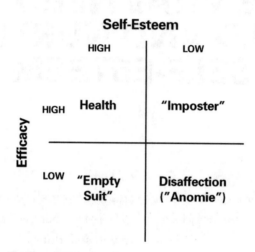

Self-esteem and efficacy compared

In the upper left is a healthy individual, who performs well and thinks well of himself or herself. (Note that we don't all perform well in everything—I'm a good writer, but I can't play a musical instrument. It's important to have efficacy in those areas important to your livelihood and profession, of course.)

The upper right is the imposter who feels he or she will be found out some day. That is, they are convinced that they aren't worth the acclaim and success they achieve, and it's only a matter of time before someone points this out and their career is over.* I believe *most* entrepreneurs experience this at one time or another, and many are trapped in it, the La Brea Tar Pits of careers.

---

*The seminal source on the topic is *The Imposter Phenomenon* by Dr. Pauline Rose Clance (Peachtree, 1985).

The lower left is the proverbial empty suit (in Texas, big hat, no cattle), who talks a good game but has no abilities. His or her self-regard is out of all proportion to their actual competence. Here you'll often find the narcissist.

Finally, the lower right is the totally disaffected. These are people who believe they have no worth and no abilities. (And if that's their self-talk, that's how they behave.) The word *anomie* means that common values and beliefs aren't accepted or don't apply. There is a type of suicide called anomic suicide at the extreme of this phenomenon.

Our need is to achieve the upper left quadrant *and remain there.**

When we perform well—and the prior nine chapters are focused on helping you to perform well quickly in your field—*and* believe in your own worth and value, we provide for the optimum chances of personal success.

Postlaunch Lesson

You can be your own best supporter or your own worst detractor. That's not much of a choice.

Aside from tests, therapeutic interventions, and the agonies of trial and error, positive self-talk is the easiest and most self-controlled route to success in this pursuit. Here's what I mean:

- When you're successful, don't say, "I was lucky." Say, "I was good and deserved that result." (You don't have to say that to others, though there's nothing wrong with that. I'm talking about true self-talk.)

- When you're not successful, don't say, "I was just awful today." Say, "We didn't make a connection, which means I could have done better."

---

* Albert Bandura, the psychologist, has probably written more lucid work on these relationships than anyone else.

- Never generalize from a specific. If you had a bad sales meeting, don't say, "I'm a terrible salesperson." Say, "That was a terrible sales meeting."

- Use perspective. Don't say, "I'll never succeed at this," but rather, "I've closed two pieces of business from five meetings, and I need to slightly improve that percentage."

- Use evidence, not supposition. Don't say, "They hate me," but reflect the facts: "They didn't make the decision to buy yet, but they haven't said no either."

- Don't unduly elevate others. Instead of saying, "He's so much better than I am in marketing," say, "He does some things better than I do that I can learn by watching him."

You're the one who talks to you more than anyone else. You're the most frequent source of feedback you'll ever have. Thus, you need to gain the discipline of positive self-talk, which I've just demonstrated. I'm not telling you to ignore setbacks or lie about your status. I *am* saying that you shouldn't be unduly harsh, focus on observed behavior and evidence, and give yourself the benefit of the doubt (as would any friend).

Script

While the customer didn't make the buying decision I had hoped for, I handled her concerns well and she agreed to another discussion, which we have scheduled. I'm going to practice that next discussion so that I can close the business at that meeting.

SUPPORT GROUPS OUTSIDE THE HOME

The ongoing support you'll need can't be solely at home (especially if you don't have a family or close friends). You need professional colleagues, more than acquaintances and less than family, to whom you can turn for support.

Here's the kind of support you should seek and you'll require:

- *Calibration of your progress:* Even if you're securing business, is it fast enough and the right kind of business?
- *Use of money:* Are you collecting fast enough, charging appropriate fees, conserving profit?
- *Quality of your work:* Are client complaints—which are inevitable—legitimate or distractions, and are you handling them well?
- *Business development:* Are you securing both solicited and spontaneous referrals, following up, and closing new business with little cost of acquisition?
- *Lifestyle:* Are you spending quality time with family and/or personal interests, or are you consumed by work?
- *Growth:* Are you getting better and better at less and less, or is your value expanding and your brand growing in repute?
- *Intellectual property:* Are you creating new and innovative approaches and models that you're protecting legally, exploiting, and publicizing?
- *Marketing prowess:* Are you engaged in promotion and market gravity in increasing ways, including print, speaking, web, networking, and so forth?
- *Support and infrastructure:* Are you securing cost-effective help in the form of vendors—printers, designers, and so on—and subcontractors who can take delivery burdens off your shoulders?
- *Strategy for growth:* Are you taking the time to step away and consider your practice and goals to adjust your current efforts toward important outcomes in your life?

This may seem like a daunting list, but it's not even exhaustive. As you grow and prosper, you'll need more and more trustworthy support to help guide your decisions. The best people to do so are often those who have been there and done that.

Let me suggest whom to rely on and whom to resist.

When I learned to ski, I had an instructor who was six yards ahead of me on the slopes doing what I sought to do, nothing more and nothing less. Some people, however, obtained what I call theoretical help—someone sitting in the chalet sipping brandy in the evening, telling them what to do when they ascended the mountain alone the next morning.

There is far too much theoretical help in our professions. In fact, there are more coaches in professional services than there are successful professional services providers. That should tell you something.

> **Postlaunch Lesson**
>
> *Along with your business growth comes your professional growth in judgment. Don't accept just anyone's opinion. Ensure that they are, themselves, experts.*

Since support structures are critical, and not all advice is sound advice, bear some rules in mind.

Alan's Rules for Maximizing Support Postlaunch

1. Professional and trade associations vary widely in their quality and contributions and must be considered carefully. Most conventions I've attended—for example, I'm one of only two people in history who is both in the National Speakers Associations Hall of Fame and a Fellow of the Institute of Management Consultants—offer little in the way of frank, valuable discussion and exchange. Unless you find talented experts *who are at levels of performance and success higher than your own at the moment,* don't feel obligated to join a professional organization, which can be more of a time dump than a growth source.

2. Social media platforms are never sources of true professional growth. They are not called business media platforms. Depending upon your profession, you might find contacts and referral points, but you won't find professional growth or consistently reliable information. Most groups on these sites are an assortment of novices trying to learn for free, or the products of people with something to sell.

3. Mastermind and similar groups can be highly effective. Usually no more than six people should participate, there should be regular (e.g., biweekly) calls or meetings, and these groups should sunset within a year at the very most.

4. Some people are experts in some fields (for example, marketing or finance) but not others (life balance or personal development). Therefore, become diverse in your selection and reliance on support resources. Unless you have a very skilled successful mentor or coach, you'll need various people's input from time to time.

5. Reciprocity will be the ultimate key. As you grow and can help others, they will help you with increasing frequency and quality. When there is mutual best interest, the assistance and support grow dramatically. And you never learn as well as when you attempt to help someone else to learn.

Let's turn to that learning in detail.

Script

Theresa, I'd like to rely on you for some financial advice in terms of the fees I collect in my business. I'm an expert on referrals, and I know your accounting firm relies on them. Would you be amenable to an occasional exchange of help with that type of reciprocity?

BUILDING EFFICACY

How do you continue to improve and grow *without* support? That is, how do your skills and competencies and talents diversify and enlarge, an important component to the self-esteem needs we discussed in earlier chapters?

Whether you're a generalist or a specialist, a realtor or a coach, you need to constantly undergo self-improvement. (I'm reminded of George Carlin's famous line, "If you're looking for self-help, why would you read a book written by somebody else?") Too often, your own improvement is prioritized just below having the car washed or mowing the lawn. It has to be raised considerably.

Postlaunch Lesson

The best investment you can possibly make, with the greatest imaginable dividends, is in yourself. Therefore, that should be the first and most consistent investment you make.

Here are the areas you should focus on, ensuring that you allocate time to investigate, learn, and integrate them into your personal set of skills:

- Technology

  What are the most efficacious ways to manage your practice, reach your prospects, manage client projects, project future needs, and so on? Never adapt technology for technology's sake, which is why you need to *pay attention to what will help you versus what will merely distract you.*

  You don't need five backup systems, but you do need to manage and segregate your lists of prospects and clients, for example. You don't need holographic imaging, but you do need the ability to meet visually online (e.g., Skype).

Pay attention to what will enhance your efficiency and invest in that. You may need to take photos without Photoshopping, and to create graphs without PowerPoint. Select what you need, not what's available.

- Content Knowledge

What do you need to stay ahead of the curve in terms of your expertise or niche? What are better ways, less expensive ways (for you) to help clients?

If you're organizing meetings, can you provide the latest in live-streaming support to augment the physical meeting? If you're providing financial services, how do the latest changes in tax codes affect people in the current and future years?

- Process Knowledge

Processes can be superimposed on any content. Think of content as *what* but process as *how*.

Do you have you a full range of decision-making skills? (For example, have you learned the specifics of identifying and managing risk?) What about planning, for you and for clients? (Do you know the differences between preventive and contingent actions?) Can you negotiate differences of opinion, resolve conflict, develop consensus agreement?

Process skills stand you in good stead in any environment and never obsolesce (decision making and problem solving have been the same for two thousand years: choose among alternatives, find the cause of your problem). No matter what your content expertise, these skills will magnify your value.

- Rules and Regulations

Some professions are government regulated (architecture, law, accounting) in terms of licensing and legal conduct. Some professions have strict canons of behavior created by associations and institutes: the American Institute of Architects and the American Bar Association, for example. And some are unregulated, yet there are best practices that can be studied: speaking, coaching, consulting.*

You should be constantly apprised of these in order to maximize your own effectiveness and to best help your clients.

Case Study

I was incorporated as a chapter C business, which in 1985 had maximum benefits for me in terms of deductions and use of my money. It did require, however, two tax returns (personal and business) and was expensive to maintain.

In the early 2000s, the government changed the tax rules, and a subchapter S was just as effective as the chapter C, but far less expensive because everything flowed through my personal return. My accountants, on top of this as well, efficiently switched me over to save me both money and time.

Another analogy: Many people switched from IRAs to Roth IRAs when the transition made sense (it didn't for everyone). Such rule changes in hiring, termination, reporting, investing, and so on occur quite frequently and can provide you with a competitive advantage if you stay abreast of them.

Building efficacy means being unafraid to try new techniques and approaches. You can't be successful long term if you're afraid to lose business or of a client being critical during a project.

In our professions, because of the laws of entropy, all plateaus erode. If you're not climbing, you're not growing. No matter how well you're

---

* For the work on my 25-year bestseller *Million Dollar Consulting* (McGraw-Hill, latest edition 2009) I found that it actually requires more licensing and approvals to be a palm reader on the boardwalk in Atlantic City than it does to be a consultant.

doing, if you coast, you will decline. Growth is not an option; it's a requirement for successful professional services practice.

Look at it in this perspective: This book is about a successful launch within 90 days. That requires tremendous growth on your part, for some of you from a standing start, but for all of you considerable acceleration. Why would you seek to discontinue that thrust or allow it to slow? There are future barriers (runners' walls) at certain growth metrics such as $500,000 and $1 million in revenues, when you must relaunch in a different way to surpass those resistance points.

So the professional growth I'm emphasizing is a lifelong need, not just the start you get out of the blocks when you begin. Thus, you might as well get good at it now.

Script

What am I doing that makes me more valuable to clients, better differentiated from competitors, more visible in a crowd? How can I invest in myself to create the dividends of continual new and repeat business with least effort and expense?

THE SUCCESS LOOP

Before we discuss a loop, take a look at the curve on the next page.

Most organizations, businesses, practices, and new ventures follow this S-curve model. If they're any good, they grow fairly steeply at the outset (which is why 90 days is plenty of time for the traction you need). However, there comes a time of slowed growth, a plateau. The time to make the leap to the next S-curve is when you have full acceleration, near the apex of the prior one.

No one in the vacuum-tube business successfully entered the transistor business that replaced it. Yet IBM has gone from punch cards to hardware to software to consulting. The former stayed on the plateau,

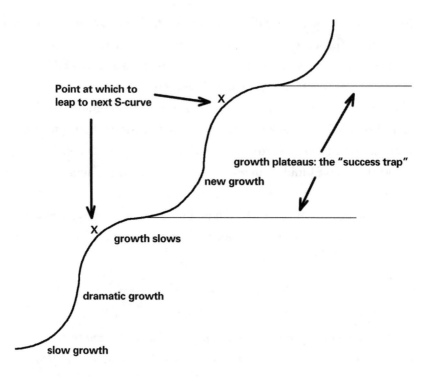

**Point at which to
leap to next S-curve** → X

growth plateaus: the "success trap"

new growth

X
growth slows

dramatic growth

slow growth

S-curve growth

which inevitably eroded. I call this the success trap. The latter kept leap-
ing to the next S-curve (and, I suspect, will continue to do so).

I've mentioned the need for reinvention and the fact that 75 percent
of my income derives from offerings not in existence three years ago.
As you move past the first three months, it's not too soon to evaluate
what your strengths *in reality and not concept* have turned out to be, and
how your passions are evolving.

Postlaunch Lesson
*Move to evolve toward a business that requires talents at
which you excel and for which you have a true passion.
Subordinate everything else.*

You must leap to the next S-curve, given your own development, technology, the economy, social mores, demographics, and so forth.* It's never too early to reinvent yourself. And the first 90 days should provide the knowledge you need to intelligently plan for this, whether immediately or in the next few months. Don't allow yourself to be inadvertently trapped in work that takes 70 percent of your time but provides only 20 percent of your income, or projects that only partially fulfill you but fill up almost all of your available time.

You can control your fate far earlier than you may currently believe.

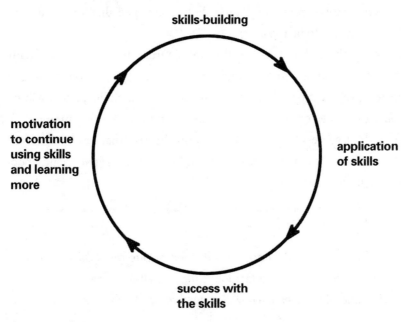

skills-building

motivation
to continue
using skills
and learning
more

application
of skills

success with
the skills

The success loop

The figure above illustrates how you can create a perpetual learning and growth model that will help you accelerate your practice and most easily leap to the next S-curve.

---

* Note that it's easiest to make the leap at the peak, where the distance is less to the next curve, than far along the plateau, where the distance is vast and the acceleration has waned.

Build your skills continually, both those you currently possess and new ones you've learned will be helpful. Apply them immediately. Don't wait to perfect them. Clients want success, not perfection. As you garner success in applying those skills, you'll gain the motivation to use them still more—to become more adept—and to acquire still more skills. This will lead you around the track yet again.

Thus: the success loop. You can create these dynamics for yourself and engage in them continually. Never allow yourself to simply learn more and more about less and less, figuratively revolving yourself into the ground like a corkscrew and winding up with the view of a frightened ostrich. There is a huge difference between a specialist and an expert. Always choose to be the latter.

Keep these charts on a wall or in a journal. Remind yourself daily that you should be climbing an S-curve and be vigilant about finding or creating the next one. Evaluate your options—in clients, relationships, colleagues, development, investment—in terms of gaining momentum around the success loop. Avoid those impediments that can create obstacles or throw sand on the tracks: unfulfilling work, negative friends, poor advice, unwise coaches.

Script

Self-script: What will I do today that will add to my skills, utilize my passion, and create acceleration to move up the S-curve or jump to a new one? Can I create a new S-curve through my own reinvention?

AVOIDING THE ROLLER COASTER BUT KEEPING THE THRILL

There are few feelings of exaltation like that slow, creaky trek up the huge, initial hill of a wooden roller coaster. You can see for miles, there's the illusion of a leisurely, controlled pace, and yet there's also the proleptic sense of the violence about to begin.

Then there's a moment between the two worlds at the apex of the hill, leading to the actual sight of an 80-degree dive and the sensation of your stomach achieving true free-fall as you plunge. There's a brief respite as the coaster soars up the next hills, but now there's little time to relax or contemplate the surroundings.

I used to get the same reaction to the giant plunges in the water, especially at the Atlantis Resort in the Bahamas, which features 90-degree water leaps. Of course, once at the bottom you can contemplate what seemed like utter chaos a few seconds earlier.

You don't need to be on a roller coaster in your profession. I've found that too many people create their own, not enjoying the few moments at the height and dreading being marooned at the bottom (feast or famine). You deserve the thrill of the ride, but you can design your own course because yours isn't dependent on gravity, or gears, or chains, or brakes.

Yours is dependent on your talent and discipline.

Inertia is the quality bestowed upon an object at rest to stay at rest or an object in motion to stay in motion. But we've established that even motion on a plateau isn't very positive, since all plateaus eventually erode. A better example would be motion in space, because an object in motion in space never stops of its own accord because space is frictionless. So long as other obstacles are avoided, the object will perpetually be in motion.

You need the power to create your own motion and the ability to steer, change course, and deliberately slow down on occasion. Fortunately, you can achieve this if you follow the advice in this book, especially the following key perpetual-motion points:

- Every day you should be moving forward, no matter how slightly. Call a referral source, write a blog post, create a new graphic, visit a prospect, network at a meeting. If you do a little every day, you will accomplish a great deal by the end of the month. Think of this as compound interest, because you'll create great heft from small deposits. (A 300-page book can be read in a month at just 10 pages a day, or a week at 40 pages a day. Same principle.)

- Your brand power should be an ongoing focus. Use your name and/or your brand names in every possible instance. The more people associate you with their needs, the less your cost of acquisition (friction) as they come to you, and the less concern there will be with credibility and fees (acceleration).

Postlaunch Lesson

You create your own ride in your profession. You can break the laws of physics by creating a perpetual-motion machine through your own branding and promotional efforts. You can't beat that for a thrill ride.

- Eliminate brakes and sand on the tracks. Build your self-esteem and assemble a support system of friends and colleagues who will help you sustain it. Stop self-editing and searching for perfection. Focus on *movement* and fine-tuning as you go. Unlike the roller coaster, you can change the speed and direction when necessary. You will never gain momentum if you hesitate at every hill, every decision.

- Adopt a mindset of helping others, not selling. Awake with the inherent knowledge (and self-talk) that you have tremendous value with which to help others, not that you're trying to find business to pay the bills. Adjust your attitude whenever necessary to reflect the fact that you'd be remiss not to try to improve others' conditions with your value, so that reaching out to them and meeting with them and entering into engagements with them is the logical result of that pursuit.

- Never stop innovating and growing. The best way to deal with volatility in the world is to use it, becoming volatile yourself in the sense of ongoing change and improvement. Don't be satisfied with doing things well; seek to do them better and better. The key is to be different to the extent that you're not comparable, not a commodity, not subject to competition, but a unique and singular resource.

- Finally, truly wear the mantle of an expert. Don't allow yourself to be portrayed—or, worse, for you to portray yourself—in an arbitrary title and role. See yourself as someone with vast expertise that can be accessed and disseminated in a wide variety of ways. View the accelerant curve as an opportunity to provide both ease of access to your value but also intimate and high-value means to access it.

Final Script

There is nothing stopping me from creating apparent and pragmatic value to others, which they can access in a variety of ways. My goal is to provide as many people as possible—directly or remotely, assertively or passively—with that value in order to improve their personal and/or business conditions. I expect and will charge equitable compensation for that value, which I will employ to help myself and my family, and thereby help others even more. That is my perpetual motion and evergreen approach to clients and customers, and I can easily see the fruits of that labor within the first 90 days of the commencement of my practice.

And here's to every 90 days getting better and better!

Appendix

SAMPLE PROPOSAL

Situation

Since becoming executive vice president for XXXXXXXX four months ago, you have discovered numerous strengths in the organization, as well as critical barriers to success. These qualities are even more significant given the goal of growing the business at a rate significantly above the historical. While doing so, you are expected to maintain the culture of the organization that is deemed valuable and productive by both your superiors and subordinates.

Your success depends upon the creation and successful implementation of a powerful strategy through an organization with the right people in the right roles acting in concert with one another. Past success in building successful relationships with clients and peers will serve you well. However, in this role, you must manage a larger and more diverse organization than before. Further, you have a finite amount of time to demonstrate that you are the right person to lead the organization at this time.

Objectives

1. Provide a professional, external sounding board for you.

2. Develop and implement an integration process to accelerate your success as the executive vice president.

3. Provide a professional, expert view of the talent at the top of the organization.

4. Develop a clear, compelling strategy.

5. Develop and use a simple though powerful implementation plan.

6. Increase the cooperation and collaboration among the top leaders to ensure attainment of the goals. Specifically, reduce the friction between two of the executive committee members, whose talents are each needed to achieve success.

Measures of Success

1. Agreement between XXXXXXXX and yourself regarding the specific outcomes for which you are accountable.

2. Reduced time to make and increased confidence in decisions.

3. Increase in revenue while maintaining profit margin

4. Evidence that the strategy and goals are clear and that behaviors are aligned in support of the plans. Such evidence will include:

   a. Spontaneous conversations that indicate such
   b. Increased cooperation
   c. Increase in the number of ideas that come from the lower levels of the organization to the top

5. Decrease in the number of conversations needed to manage the conflict at the top

6. Positive feedback from the chief operating officer regarding your performance, both financial and leadership

Value

1. Increase in sales of $1.5 million over last year will add $300,000 to net profit, taking the total net profit to $1.3 million.

2. Decrease in conflict at the top level will reduce time spent in conversation with those involved.

3. Decrease in time to market of new ideas or approaches.

4. Acceleration of your ability to make positive impact.

5. Create a useful framework for decision making, reducing time to do so.

Method and Options

Option 1

For a period of six months, conduct face-to-face meetings with you as needed and provide unlimited telephone consultation.

Meet with each of your direct reports to more fully understand them and the organizational context.

Conduct a meeting of the direct report team to debrief observations and further accelerate your integration.

Meet with the executive committee to ensure clarity of purpose and goals and alignment. Create a strategic framework to ensure the attainment of growth and profitability goals.

Meet with you and XXXXXXXX to resolve the issues between them and among the three of you.

Meet with you and XXXXXXXX to establish goals and expectations, and to achieve alignment and support for your plans.

Option 2

All the elements of Option 1, plus:

A follow-up meeting of the direct report group at the five-month mark, to identify new opportunities, challenges, and ideas, and solidify your leadership.

Option 3

All the elements of Options 1 and 2 and:

Survey the entire organization to more thoroughly understand the context and any cultural barriers to the effective implementation of your strategy. Analysis and debrief of results with the direct report team included.

Timing

The initial interviews and meetings will be completed within eight weeks of the commencement of this project.

The consultation to you and the executive committee will continue for a total of six months.

Joint Accountabilities

XXXXXXXX will provide Constance Dierickx, PhD as the project leader. She will be continually involved in all aspects of the project, and will serve as the primary contact with XXXXXXXX. We will sign non-disclosure agreements as requested, and all work contents remain the property of XXXXXXXX.

XXXXXXXX will provide us with reasonable access to key management people, documentation, and company information, as appropriate, within the time frames outlined above. XXXXXXXX will be responsible for scheduling of meetings, obtaining necessary facilities, equipment, and related support for meetings. XXXXXXXX agrees to the fee structure outlined below and will adhere to the reimbursement of expenses procedures as specified.

Terms and Conditions

Option 1: $60,000

Option 2: $70,000

Option 3: $85,000

Payment terms are one-half fee due upon the signing of this letter of agreement and one-half due 45 days hence.

Reasonable travel and living expense are submitted monthly as accrued, at cost, and payment is due upon receipt of the invoice.

This project is noncancelable, and agreed-upon payment terms are due as described. You may postpone or delay any part of the work as you deem necessary. The quality of our work is guaranteed. If we do not meet your objectives, as stated above, we will refund your fee.

ACCEPTANCE

Speaking contract

This represents an agreement between the Acme Company and Summit Consulting Group, Inc., as represented by Alan Weiss. Alan Weiss will conduct a half-day workshop for Acme at a site of its choosing on March 10, 2004, from approximately 8:30 a.m. to noon.

The session title is "Million Dollar Selling: How to Increase the Size of Any Sale at Any Time." The audience will comprise about 40 senior salespeople and sales managers. Alan Weiss will provide the proprietary intellectual property, audio/visual aids, handouts, and facilitation. Acme will provide the site, administrative support, scheduling, refreshments, and equipment (overhead projector and screen, two easels with pads and markers, a wireless lapel microphone). John Davis, vice president of sales, will introduce the session that morning.

There are three options available to you for this session:

1. We will conduct the session as described, and create relevant examples and exercises based on our discussions prior to it.

2. We will interview five sales managers and five salespeople, read current proposals, and talk to three customers to use this information to create case studies and live application.

3. We will interview as above, send an electronic survey to all participants, talk to customers as above, and talk to three prospects who did not buy your services to create a comprehensive group analysis of current practices and enable the group to immediately build our sales techniques into current prospecting activities on a real-time basis. *Note that this approach would require a full day's workshop.*

The fee for option 1 is $7,500; for option 2 is $9,500, and for option 3 is $12,000. A 50 percent deposit is required to hold the date and for us to begin designing the day. The balance is due at the presentation itself.

Alternatively, you may avail yourself of a 10 percent discount by paying the full fee in advance. Expenses will be charged as actually accrued and will be due upon presentation of our invoice subsequent to the session.

Please indicate which option you'd prefer, sign this agreement below, and enclose the appropriate payment.

Thank you for the opportunity to work with you on this important development project. Please feel free to call at any time to further customize the approaches.

For Summit Consulting Group, Inc.:   For Acme Company:

Alan Weiss, President   Title:_____

Date:_____

Subcontractor Agreement

The provisions in this document will govern our relationship while Joan Larson conducts work on behalf of Summit Consulting Group, Inc., at the Acme Company.

1. You will identify yourself as a subcontractor for Summit Consulting Group, Inc. You will not hand out personal business cards or talk about your personal practice at any time.

2. You will do no promotion for your personal business at any time.

3. You will implement according to instructions provided by Summit Consulting Group, Inc., and will not agree to any altered, modified, or new conditions with the client. Any such client requests will be passed on to Alan Weiss for decision.

4. Your expenses will be reimbursed monthly, within 10 days of receipt. You will turn in expenses on the last day of the month. Reimbursement will include airfare at discounted coach rates, taxis, meals (not to exceed $75 per day), hotel room at the Marriott Downtown, and tips. All other expenses, including phone, recreation, laundry, etc., are not reimbursable.

5. Your payment rate will be $1,500 per day on-site, and $750 per day off-site, as directed and approved by Summit Consulting Group, Inc. You agree that the work assigned to you will be completed within 60 days, with a cap of 15 actual days on-site and a cap of 4 days off-site. You will complete the work below, even if it requires additional days, but payment will cap at the levels noted:

    - Conduct 12 focus groups as assigned for 90 minutes each
    - Analyze and produce reports on each group in progress
    - Analyze and produce a report for the total group experience
    - Meet with Alan Weiss at the conclusion to discuss the final report
        Fees will be paid within 10 days of the submission of your time reports at the conclusion of each month, providing that all individual focus group progress reports have been submitted.

6. All work created and all materials provided you are the sole property of Summit Consulting Group, Inc. You may not cite this organization as your client in conversation or in writing, and all communications with Summit Consulting Group, Inc., and Acme are confidential and subject to the nondisclosure agreement you have signed.

7. You will conduct yourself professionally, observe business ethics and courtesy, and meet the work requirements above. Failure to do so in the opinion of Acme and/or Summit Consulting Group, Inc., will result in termination of this agreement and cessation of payment.

Your notarized signature below indicates full agreement and compliance with these requirements:

_____Notary, including signature, date, and seal:

Joan Larson

Date: _____

Inquiry to Speak at Trade Association Conference

I'm proposing that I speak at your conference on May 6 in San Diego with a presentation entitled "How to Avoid a Strategy That Sits on the Shelf: *Why Planning Is Killing Strategy*." This is designed to fit well with the conference theme of "Searching the Future."

Among other advantages, the participants would benefit from:

- Specific tools to create a strategy of inclusion
- Alignment of all individual objectives behind corporate goals
- Separation of strategy (top down) and planning (bottom up)
- Acquisition of a template to apply immediately
- Clear methods to use strategy as a real-time management tool
- Real-world case studies to provide practice and discussion

I'm the author of 17 articles and position papers on strategy and strategic initiatives, several of which are in the enclosed press kit. My work has included strategy retreats with Acme Corp., Bravo Institute, and Charlie, Inc., all of which are about the same size as most of your member organizations. In addition, I've enclosed an audiotape of several radio interviews I've provided on the subject, as well as a video of my presentation to the Minnesota State Bankers Conference on "Strategy As a Leadership Leverage Point." You'll also find several testimonials related to this topic and my overall presentation effectiveness in the package.

I'll call you on Friday, February 6 at 10 a.m. your time to discuss this further. If you would like to talk before then, use any of the contact points on this letterhead to reach me.

Thanks in advance for your consideration. I'm looking forward to our discussion.

Qualifying Leads

It's important to be able to quickly qualify prospects and leads so that we can apply scarce resources and time to the highest potential opportunities. Therefore, you need to create some qualifying criteria.

On the next page is a model I've developed. Substitute your own criteria and ratings as appropriate. I've filled in the content to illustrate the usage. It's a great idea to run every prospective client through this quickly. (Just because you only have a few leads doesn't mean you should pursue them if they're not potentially valuable. You'd be better off spending the time on further marketing.)

Instructions:

1. List your ideal traits for a potential client.

2. Rate those traits based on 10 as highest and 1 as lowest. You may have more than one 10 or any other number.

3. Fill in the actual traits that your prospect possesses.

4. Score your prospect's actual traits against each ideal, with a 10 being a perfect fit, and a 0 being a total mismatch.

5. Multiply the rating times the score in each category.

6. Add up the rated scores to get a total.

7. Compare the total against the ideal total (all 10s in scoring) and come up with a percentage of the idea.

8. Decide which percentage minimum is required for follow-up and with what priority and apply. I recommend nothing below 80 percent.

Note: If you don't have enough information to complete the form, do some further homework. It will be worth it.

In my example, the maximum R/S possible (all scores of 10 in every category) would be 420. The actual candidate scored 338, which is 80 percent, or a low B.

Alan's Promotional Potholes

Failure to use compelling words and phrases: "We assist in growth …" is weak compared to "We are your partner in dramatic growth …"

Lack of third-party testimonials and support: It's much more effective to allow someone else to tell your story.

Degrading others rather than elevating yourself: don't disparage the competition ... ignore them.

Inconsistent promotion: Your brand, value proposition, values, and messages must be uniform and consistently applied across electronic media, press kits, collateral material, conversation, speeches, third-party references.

Associating yourself with names as if osmosis will promote you: Being in a book with famous authors or sharing a media event for a fee with experts only impresses the people who cashed your check for the dubious distinction.

The belief that your message is sufficient: Aphorisms, affirmations, and adages all cool in the noonday sun. You must bring pragmatic ideas that demonstrably improve people.

Ignoring the true, economic buyer: Promoting to nonbuyers, gate-keepers, and intermediaries is a waste of marketing money and time.

Being inarticulate in your own value and outcomes: Most speakers and consultants become tongue-tied if they're doing anything beyond describing their own methodology. But you must answer this question, "What's in it for the buyer?"

Conformance: Everyone has the same video, the same stories, the same coaches, the same web design. *Boring.* You're better off being an imperfect original than a perfect copy.

Lack of long-term focus: You must promote daily, consistently, and relentlessly. Every highly successful person you meet in the business is constantly promoting and marketing. Think about it.

Invoice for Expense Reimbursement

SUMMIT CONSULTING GROUP

Box 1009

East Greenwich, RI

02818-0964

Tel (401) 884-2778

Fax (401) 884-5068

Date: January 15, 20XX   No. 2141

For coach airfare, per agreement, in connection with keynote speech at CAPS national convention, November 2011.

Total Due: $800.00 US

Terms: Due upon receipt

Payable only in US funds drawn on a US bank or by wire transfer

Thank You!

XXXXXXXX

Canadian Association of Professional Speakers

Our Federal ID number is 22-2458120

Our courier address is 85 Brisas Circle, East Greenwich, RI 02818

Invoice for consulting project

Box 1009   Tel (401) 884-2778

East Greenwich, RI

02818-0964   Fax (401) 884-5068

Date: March 3, 20XX   No. 116

For the team-building project described in our proposal of January 31, including design, delivery, discussions, and follow-up as specified:

$55,000

Terms: 50% due on commencement, 50% due in 45 days

Total Due: $27,500

Terms: Due upon receipt

Thank You!

John Wilbur

Executive Vice President

Acme Explosives Company

Our Federal ID number is 22-2458120

Our courier address is 85 Brisas Circle, East Greenwich, RI 02818

Inquiry Letter to the Editor

I'm writing to suggest an article for *Today's Banker* entitled, "Selling at the Retail Level: You Don't Get If You Don't Ask." The previously unpublished piece would rely on my work with Citibank, Bank of America, and JP Morgan Chase at the branch level.

Specifically, your readers would learn:

- How to provide tellers with the tools to prompt new accounts
- How to create need through questioning
- How to direct customers to platform officers for the close
- How to create and use point-of-transaction sales tools

I've helped clients achieve 25 percent and higher new sales of products and services over prior years, *despite the economy*. There are testimonial letters enclosed from several customers—among your readers, I'm sure—who attest to these dramatic results.

As with many of your articles, there will be mini-interviews included, as well as illustrations of the materials cited. I can write the piece to your specifications and have it to you within 14 days of your approval.

My work has been published in *Management Weekly, Financial Matters,* and *Branch Banking News,* among two dozen other periodicals; I've appeared several times on CNN-FN to comment on sales in tough times, and I'm currently working on a book for AMACOM called *How to Make the Sale the First Time, Every Time.*

I've enclosed an SASE, and have also forwarded this same letter by e-mail, in case it's easier for you to respond in that manner. Thanks in advance for your kind consideration.

Acknowledgments

I want to thank the people in my Super Coaching Program (KAATN: Kick Ass and Take Names) who prove that no one learns more than the coach.

Great appreciation to my daughter, Danielle, independent TV producer, and son, Jason, actor/director/teacher, for their inspired pursuit of the arts and my further involvement in that quest.

Thanks to my twin granddaughters, Alaina and Gabrielle, who no doubt will critique this book once they find they can't color in it.

And for my lovely wife of 45 years who is often called by her friends "the long-suffering" but whom I refer to more briefly as Maria.

Index

Accelerant Curve, 143–146, 221, 191–194
Accelerated movement, 192
Accountants, 28–29
Acquisition
  in alliance apportionment, 120, 121
  of clients, 73–86
Adjectives, 53
Advice
  brain trust for, 35
  on forum, 36–37
  good intentioned people giving, 61–62
  investors giving, 63
  nonknowing people giving, 61–62
  projectionists giving, 62
  unsolicited, 35–37
Advisor, 9
Alan's Blog, 94–95
AlansForums.com, 92, 104
Alliance apportionment, 120–121
Amazon.com, 168
Anomie, 206, 207
Apple, 157
Apps, 157
Arrogance, 53
Art students, 30

Aruba, 179
Atlantis Resort, 219
Attorneys
  corporation, 21–22
  expectations of, 23–24
  family of, 177
  IP, 22
  litigator, 22
  need for, 21–24
  overview of, 21–24
  proposals handled by, 23
  services of, 23–24
  types of, 21–24
Attribution, 22
Audio, 164–165
Avocation
  definition of, 46–47
  occupation and, 46–49
  overview of, 46–47

Bahamas, 219
Balance
  OOI and, 173–176
  overview of, 197–199
  people and, 173–176
  perspective in, 198–199
Bankers
  credit and, 12
  definition of, 9

Banks. *See also* Finances
  cash in, 201
  contacts in, 13
  credit cards and, 160
  investing with, 185
  relationships with, 185
Barr, Chad, 91
Bartered services, 88, 129
Beach, 179
Behavior
  of experts, 194–195
  factors, 61–64
Bills, paying, 128–129, 183–184
Black book, 7–8
Blogs
  Alan's, 94–95
  categories on, 95–96
  creating and exploiting, 94–97
  frequency of, 96
  as idiosyncratic, 95–96
  OOI, 175
  perspective and, 96
  points about, 96
  responsiveness of, 96
Bookkeeper, 28–29
Booklets, 167–168
Boston University, 177
Bounce factors, 144–145
Boutique consulting, 50
Boutique firms, subcontracting for, 79
Brain trust, 35
Brands
  building, 40

consulting, 39–40
contrarian, 39–40
creating, 39–42
equity, 40
as focus, 220
imperative, 197
name as, 39, 149–152
passive income and, 197
power, 220
pyramid, 41
quality represented by, 40–42
questions, 40–41
Breakfast meetings, gravity, 58
Bridges
  guidelines for, 5–6
  importance of, 9–10
  maintaining, 3–7
  military campaign and, 5
  solo practitioners and, 5
Broadcasting
  case study, 153–154
  lessons, 155
  services, 152–158
Business
  ethic, 48–49
  media platforms, 91
  parachute, 145, 194
  small, 122
  transistor, 215–216
  trip, 178
  vacuum-tube, 215–216
Buyer contact, 67–70
Buyers. *See* Clients; Prospects

Calendar, 31–33, 177
Call-everyone-you-know list, 74
Cash
    in bank, 201
    payment with, 88, 89
    reserve, 201
Cash flow problems, 128
Chapter C business, 214
Child, 3
Clance, Pauline Rose, 206
Clients. *See also* Ideal customer
    acquisition of, 73–86
    case study, 77
    definition of, 8
    employer as, 73–74
    finding, 73–86
    first, 73–76
    in first 30 days, 73–90
    meeting, 133
    nonprofit as, 74–77
    template for, 83–85
    traits of, 83–86
*Close Encounters of the Third
    Kind*, 81
Clubs, 65, 77
Cold calls, 113
Colleagues, 182–183
Collection, 127–129
Collector, 159–160
Commitments
    exercise for, 126–127
    to self, 126–127
Communities
    creating, 91–92

groups, 65
    progression influencing, 91–92
Compound interest, 219
Computer, as equipment, 25–26
Conference room, 136
Confidence, 53
Conservative lifestyle, 202
Consultants
    experts and, 146–149
    subcontracting for, 79
Consulting
    boutique, 50
    brand, 39–40
Consumer evangelism, 157
Consumer service operation, social
    media used in, 99–100
Contacts
    in bank, 13
    black book with, 7–8
    categories of, 8–9, 10
    consolidating, 7–10
    definition of, 5
    Harvard graduate with, 7–8
    high, 10
    low, 10
    medium, 10
    organizing, 8–10
    priority of, 10
    on social media, 132
    streams of influence and, 113
    syncing, 132
Content knowledge, 213
Contingency fees, 88
Contrarian, 39–40, 174–175

Copier, as equipment, 26
Corporations
  attorney, 21–22
  early appointment for, 136
  ideal time for, 136
  limited liability, 22
  subchapter S, 22
Credibility
  buyer contact and, 67–68
  horn-blowing and, 56
  questions, 67–68
  website influencing, 100–104
Credit
  bankers and, 12
  definition of, 9
Credit cards, 26, 88, 160, 202
Customer. *See* Clients; Ideal
    customer
Cyberspace. *See* Internet

Data, 148
Dawkins, Richard, 156
Debt
  avoiding, 186
  credit-card, 202
  as intelligent, 11–12
  investing and, 186
  using, 11–12
Degrees of interaction, 192–193
Delivering
  in alliance apportionment,
    120, 121
  marketing while, 115–118
  promises, 125–127

scope creep in, 116, 117
  scope seep in, 117
Design
  finances and, 28–31
  local finances and, 28–31
  support, 31
Designers, 29–31
Digital empire
  definition of, 91
  summary of, 129–133
Direct mail, 113
Disaffected, 206, 207
Documents, 162
Downloads, 196
Dropbox, 132
Dun & Bradstreet, 153–154

E-books, 161–162
Efficacy
  building, 212–215
  self-esteem compared with,
    206–207
Egos, 66
E-mail
  accepting, 131
  signature, 132
Emotional support, 199–202
Employer
  as client, 73–74
  former, 73–74
  phone meeting with, 74
  as prospect, 73–74
Empty suit, 206, 207
Enrichment night, 77

Environmental factors, 61–64
Equipment
    computer as, 25–26
    copier as, 26
    credit card terminal as, 26
    furniture as, 27
    phone as, 24–25
    postage, 26
    storage, 27–28
    supplies and, 24–28
Errors and omissions insurance, 13
Evangelists, 53
Expense reimbursement, 128–129
Expenses
    investing for, 184
    saving for, 184
Expertise
    clear, 195
    downloading, 165
    focusing on, 194–195
    overview of, 194–195
Experts
    Accelerant Curve and, 221
    behavior of, 194–195
    calling oneself, 6–7, 146–149, 221
    case study, 153–154
    consultant and, 146–149
    definition of, 153
    efficacy of, 154
    expertise disseminated by,
        146–147
    as label, 6–7, 146–149, 221
    1% Solution regarding, 148
    reason for, 6–7, 146–149

role of, 146–149
    as support, 211
    value enhanced by, 147–149, 221
    in value propositions, 147

Facebook, 92, 99–100
Failures, causes of, 10–13
Family
    of attorney, 177
    gifts from, 202
    help, 202
    investors, 63
    marketing and, 78
    money from, 202
    as ongoing help, 187
    as support, 202
    vacations needed by, 176–178
Fax number, 25
FedEx, 26
Feedback
    for colleagues, 182
    myth about, 35–36
    projection in, 36
    unsolicited, 35–37
Fees
    contingency, 88
    gravity and, 56
    horn-blowing and, 56
Feet on street, 157
Finances
    building, 10–13
    design and, 28–31
    exercise, 11–12
    issues, 10–13

Finances (*Cont.*)
  local, 28–31
  support, 11–13, 31
  tactics, 11–13
Financial advisor, need for, 13
Financial experts, 28–31
First 90 days
  ideal prospects in, 109–112
  vacations during, 178
  viral marketing in, 158
First 30 days
  clients in, 73–90
  summary of, 59–60
Fishing gear, 160
Flash drive, 167
Flexibility, 32
Ford, Henry, 11
Former employer, 73–74
Forum, 36–37
Francis, Colleen, 133
Free marketing, 76–79
Full life, 197–199
Furniture, as equipment, 27

Gage, Randy, 173–174
Gear, 160
Gene, 156
Generalists, 43
Gifts, 202
Godin, Seth, 101
Goldfayn, Alex, 112
Goldsmith, Marshall, 54
Good intentioned people, 61–62
Gooding, Cuba, Jr., 119

Grand resignation, 4
Graphics designers, 29–31
Gravity
  appeal of, 67–70
  breakfast meetings, 58
  fees and, 56
  networking, 58
  overview of, 56–59
  publishing, 58, 69
  referrals, 57, 69
  routes, 56–59, 68–69
  speaking, 58, 69
  techniques, 56–59, 68–69
  from Web, 69
  wheel, 68–69
Growth
  continuous, 220–221
  model, 215–218
  need for, 214–215
  S-curve, 215–218
  stopping, 220–221

Hang 10, 110
Hard-copy value
  booklets providing, 167–168
  flash drive providing, 167
  manuals providing, 167
  newsletters providing,
    166–167
  overview of, 166–168
  passive income provided by,
    166–168
Harvard graduate, 7–8
Healthy individual, 206, 207–208

Help
 family, 202
 ongoing, 186–189
 theoretical, 210
High, 10
High tech, 104–107, 196
High touch, 104–107, 196
Home
 equity loans, 201
 finding, 13–16
 as office, 13–15
 support outside, 208–211
 working from, 13–15
Home page, 101–102
Horn-blowing, 52–56, 66–67
Hosting, 196
Hot spot, 157–158
Humility, 52–56, 66–67
Hype, on website, 103

IBM, 215–216
Ideal clients. *See* Ideal customers
Ideal conditions
 in ideal mate, 137–139
 methods for, 138
 summary of, 137–139
Ideal customers, 83–86
 Accelerant Curve for, 143–146
 ideal manner for, 135–136
 in ideal mate, 134–135
 ideal place for, 137
 ideal time for, 136
 list of, 135
 overview of, 134–135

Ideal manner
 for ideal customers, 135–136
 in ideal mate, 135–136
 overview of, 135–136
Ideal mate
 ideal conditions in, 137–139
 ideal customers in, 134–135
 ideal manner in, 135–136
 ideal place in, 137
 ideal time in, 136
 summary of, 133–139
Ideal place
 for ideal customers, 137
 in ideal mate, 137
 overview of, 137
Ideal prospects, 83–86
 criteria for, 111–112, 123
 in first 90 days, 109–112
 focusing on, 109
 market value bell curve, 109–112,
  123–124
 retail, 122–124
 schematic for, 109–112
 wholesale, 122–124
Ideal time
 for corporations, 136
 for ideal customers, 136
 in ideal mate, 136
 overview of, 136
Imposter, 206
The Imposter Phenomenon
  (Clance), 206
Individual Retirement Accounts
  (IRAs), 214

Inertia, 219–221
Inferiority, 67
Influencers, 113–115
Information, 148
Innovation, 220–221
Inputs, 44
Insurance
  agent, 13
  errors and omissions, 13
  liability, 13
Intellectual property (IP)
  attorney, 22
  attribution, 22
  definition of, 52
  as public, 22
  in sweet spot, 52
  trademarks protecting, 53
Interaction, 192–193
Interest, 219
Internal Revenue Service (IRS), 129
Internet. *See also* Web presence
  business perspective of, 91–94
  contacts enabled by, 133
  limiting use of, 130–132
  navigation, 129–133
  rules for, 93–94
  time, 130–132
  upsides and downsides, 91–94
Investing
  with banks, 185
  debt and, 186
  for expenses, 184
  overdraft protection and, 185–186
  overview of, 183–186

  for retirement, 184
  slush fund, 184–185
  wisely, 183–186
Investors
  advice given by, 63
  family, 63
IP. *See* Intellectual property
IRAs. *See* Individual Retirement
    Accounts
IRS. *See* Internal Revenue Service

Jerry Maguire, 119

Knowledge, 148–149, 213
Krzyzewski, Mike, 152

Leadership roles, 175
Leads
  collecting, 81
  creating and qualifying, 82–86
  importance of, 81
  organizing, 82
  in pipeline, 80–82
  quality, 82–86
  return on, 82–86
  sources of, 81
  template for, 83–85
  true, 82
Learned Optimism (Seligman), 205
Letterhead, 27
Leverage, payment influenced by,
    88–89
Liability insurance, 13
Licensing, 196

Life balance. *See* Balance
Lifestyle, 202
Limited liability corporation
    (LLC), 22
LinkedIn, 100, 132
Lists, 167
LISTSERV, 163
Litigator, 22
LLC. *See* Limited liability
    corporation
Loans, 201–202
Local finances, 28–31
Local merchants, paying,
    128–129
Location, choosing, 13–16
Logo, 30
Lousy relationships, 200
Low, 10

Maister, David, 61
Malpractice insurance. *See* Errors
    and omissions insurance
Manuals, 167
Margin, 86
Market gravity. *See* Gravity
Market value bell curve, 109–112,
    123–124
Marketing. *See also* Pipelines; Viral
    marketing
  case study, 78, 79
  delivering while, 115–118
  family and, 78
  focus, 117–118
  for free, 76–79

importance of, 39
provocation in, 78
publishing, 78
speaking, 77
word-of-mouth, 59
Mastermind groups, 65, 211
Media
  business platforms, 91
  contacting, 175
  definition of, 9
  OOI and, 175
Medium, 10
Megatrends (Naisbitt), 104
Meme, 156
Mental set, 48–49, 220
Merck, 87
Methodology, 45–46, 120, 121, 151
Microsoft, 88
Military campaign, 5
Mindset. *See* Mental set
Mini-manuals, 162
Money. *See also* Investing
  collecting, 127–129
  concerns about, 200–201
  from family, 202
  from home equity loan, 201
  lifestyle influencing, 202
  liquid, 185
  from loans, 201–202
  relationships and, 200–202
  from retirement funds, 201
  from savings, 201
  spouses on, 200–201
  temptations, 183

Motion, 219–221
Movement, on Accelerant Curve,
   191–192

Naisbitt, John, 104
Names. *See also* Contacts
   as brand, 39, 149–152
   collecting, 81
   dropping, 54
   at formal events, 151
   introducing, 151
   on methodology, 151
   on publishing, 151
   repetition of, 151–152
   in third person, 151
Nephew, 200
Networking, gravity, 58
Newsletters, 162–163,
   166–167
Noncash offers, 88
Nonknowing people, 61–62
Nonleads, 82
Nonprofit, 74–77
Norwegian stamps, 159–160
Notifications, 131

Object of Interest (OOI), 69–70,
   157–158, 173–176
Objective apportionment, 121
Occupation
   avocation and, 46–49
   definition of, 47–48
   overview of, 47–48
Offerings, 193–195

Office
   environment, 14–15
   external options, 15–16
   home as, 13–15
   of professionals, 15
   renting, 15–16
   shared suites as, 16
   wife on, 14
1% Solution, 148
Ongoing help, 186–189
OOI. *See* Object of Interest
Outputs, 44–45
Overdraft protection, 185–186
Overwhelm, 64

Panic, 63–64
Parachute business, 145, 194
Paradigms, 48–49
Partnerships, 119–121
Passive income
   brand and, 197
   case study, 161
   example, 159
   hard-copy value providing,
     166–168
   overview of, 195–197
   remote coaching providing,
     169–171
   subscription services providing,
     162–165
   Web-based products and services
     providing, 159–162
Patterson, James, 174
Paul (saint), 157

Payment
  bartering services as, 88, 129
  of bills, 128–129, 183–184
  case study, 87
  with cash, 88, 89
  cash flow problems delaying,
    128
  collecting, 127–128
  at conclusion, 88
  with credit cards, 88
  issues, 88–89
  leverage influencing, 88–89
  noncash offers as, 88
  of ongoing help, 188
  overview of, 86–89, 127–128
  to self, 183
  subcontracting, 188
  terms, 86–88, 127–128, 188
Peer influencers. *See* Influencers
Peer-to-peer direct referrals,
    112–115
People
  balance and, 173–176
  categories of, 8–9
  drawing, 173–176
  good intentioned, 61–62
  nonknowing, 61–62
  as ongoing help, 187–189
  OOI influencing, 173–176
  promises made by, 125–127
Perpetual motion, 219–221
Perspective
  in balance, 198–199
  blogs and, 96

Phone
  employer meeting on, 74
  as equipment, 24–25
  return calls, 118
Picasso, Pablo, 66
Pipelines
  creating, 80–82
  definition of, 80
  leads in, 80–82
Plateau, 219
Podcasts, 160–161, 164–165
Postage, 26
PR. *See* Public relations
Premature panic, 63–64
Print, 162–163
Prior employer. *See* Former
    employer
Private time, public time and,
    64–66
Pro bono work, 74–77
Process knowledge, 213
Productivity, guidelines for,
    33–34
Professionals
  definition of, 9
  groups, 65, 70, 77, 210
  office space of, 15
  speaking to, 77
  as support, 210
Progression, 91–92
Projection, 36
Projectionists, 62
Promises, 125–127
Proposals, attorneys handling, 23

Prospects. *See also* Ideal prospects
   case study, 77
   definition of, 9
   employer as, 73–74
   nonprofit as, 74–77
   sequence for, 75–76
   with streams of influence,
     112–115
   template for, 83–85
   tips, 76
   traits of, 83–86
   warm, 73–74
Provocation, 54, 78
Public relations (PR), 9
Public time, private time and,
   64–66
Publishing
   gravity, 58, 69
   marketing, 78
   name placed on, 151
   OOI, 175

Quality
   brand representing, 40–42
   circles, 40
   leads, 82–86

Real estate, website as, 100–104
Realism, 32
Recommenders, 113
Reference sources, 9
Referrals
   gravity, 57, 69
   peer-to-peer direct, 112–115
Regulations, 213–214

Reimbursement, 128–129
Relationships
   with banks, 185
   download, 196
   exorcising, 200
   hosting, 196
   licensing, 196
   lousy, 200
   money and, 200–202
   retainer, 196
   sour, 200
   virtual, 30–31
Remote coaching, 169–171
Reserve, 201
Retail market
   definition of, 122
   ideal prospects in, 122–124
   website to, 124
   wholesale market and,
     122–124
Retail service operation. *See*
     Consumer service operation
Retainers, 196
Retirement, 184, 201
Return calls, 118
Return on leads (ROL), 82–86
Robbins, Tony, 173
ROL. *See* Return on leads
Roller coaster, 218–221
Roth Individual Retirement
     Accounts (Roth IRAs), 214
Rules, 213–214

Salespeople, humility of, 55
Savings, 201

Scheduling, 31–34
  calendar, 31–33
  with flexibility, 32
  with realism, 32
Scope creep, 116, 117
Scope seep, 117
Screen savers, 131
S-curve, 215–218
Self-esteem
  disaffected with, 206, 207
  efficacy compared with, 206–207
  empty suit with, 206, 207
  healthy individual with, 206,
    207–208
  imposter with, 206
  self-talk influencing, 205–208
Self-improvement
  content knowledge, 213
  process knowledge, 213
  regulation, 213–214
  rule, 213–214
  technology, 212–213
The Selfish Gene (Dawkins), 156
Self-talk
  overview of, 205–208
  self-esteem enhanced by,
    205–208
Seligman, Martin, 205
Serial developers, 110
Service clubs, 65
Services. *See also* Subscription
    services; Web-based products
    and services
  array of, 152–158
  broadcasting, 152–158

Shared suites, 16
Signature, 132
Skiing, 210
Skills, building, 218
Slush fund, 184–185
Small business, 122
Smugness, 53
Social media
  case study, 79
  consumer service operation using,
    99–100
  contacts on, 132
  effectiveness of, 97–100
  support provided by, 211
  time on, 98–99
  truth about, 97–100
  value offered in, 79
Solo practitioners, bridges and, 5
Sour relationships, 200
Space, 219
Speaking
  gravity, 58, 69
  marketing, 77
  to professionals, 77
Specialist, 43
Spielberg, Steven, 81
Spokes, 50–52
Spouses
  debriefing with, 181–182,
    199–200
  meeting, 181–182, 199–200
  on money, 200–201
  support of, 18–19, 199–200
Stamps, 159–160
State Street Bank, 154, 178

Steel, Danielle, 174

Storage, 27–28

Strangers, 176

Streams of influence, 112–115

Strengths, 55, 216–218

Subchapter S corporation,
22, 214

Subcontracting
for boutique firms, 79
for consultants, 79
on ongoing basis, 186–189
payment, 188
reasons for, 186–187

Subscription services
access, 165
audio, 164–165
newsletters as, 162–163
overview of, 162–165
passive income provided by,
162–165
podcast, 164–165
print, 162–163
video, 164

Success
loop, 215–218
trap, 215–216

Suicide, 207

Summit Consulting Group, 30,
149–150

Suppliers, local, 30–31

Supplies
equipment and, 24–28
FedEx, 26
letterhead as, 27
postage, 26
UPS, 26

Support
backup for, 189
colleagues as, 182–183
design, 31
diversifying, 211
emotional, 199–202
experts as, 211
family as, 202
finance, 31
gathering, 17–19
horn-blowing, 54
list of, 209
local, 30–31
mastermind groups as, 211
maximizing, 210–211
as ongoing help, 188–189
outside home, 208–211
professionals as, 210
reciprocity to, 176, 211
requirement for, 209
rules for, 210–211
social media providing, 211
of spouse, 18–19
system, 17–19
time and, 180–181
utilizing, 180–183

Sweet spot
boutique consulting, 50
definition of, 49
example, 51–52
identifying, 49–52
IP in, 52
overview of, 49–52
spokes, 50–52
sub-categories, 50–52

Syncing, 132

Technology
  high, 104–107
  self-improvement, 212–213
Teskalefbre, Rebecca Young,
  150–151
Testimonials
  getting, 103–104
  on website, 103–104
Theoretical help, 210
Third person, 151
Thought leader, 54
Thrill, 218–221
Time. *See also* Ideal time
  allocating, 180–181
  calendar and, 31–33
  choices and, 31
  Internet, 130–132
  as priority, 31, 180–181
  private, 64–66
  public, 64–66
  scheduling, 31–34
  on social media, 98–99
  support structure and, 180–181
Toll-free number, 15
Trademarks, 53
Transistor business, 215–216
True leads, 82
Twitter, 79, 100

Under-construction approach,
  102
Uniqueness, 193
United Parcel Service (UPS), 26
Unsolicited feedback, 35–37
Upgrades, 131
UPS. *See* United Parcel Service

Vacations
  Aruba, 179
  beach, 179
  business trip, added on to,
    178
  calendar for, 177
  case study, 177, 179
  family needing, 176–178
  during first 90 days, 178
  kinds of, 178
  maximizing, 176–179
  overview of, 176–179
  State Street Bank and, 178
  work during, 178–179
Vacuum-tube business,
  215–216
Value. *See also* Hard-copy value
  case study, 117
  expert enhancing, 147–149,
    221
  numbers as behind, 150
  on social media platforms,
    79
  suggesting, 117
Value propositions
  definition of, 43
  expert in, 147
  finding, 43–46
  generalists and, 43
  methodology as, 45–46
  as outputs, 44–45
  overview of, 43–46
  questions, 45–46
  specialist and, 43
Vault, 143–144
Video, 164

Viral marketing, 59
  Apple using, 157
  in first 90 days, 158
  overview of, 156–158
  Paul using, 157
Virals
  definition of, 156
  overview of, 156–158
Virtual relationships, 30–31
Volatility, 220–221

Web presence, 54, 69. *See also*
    Digital empire
Web-based products and services
  case study, 161
  documents as, 162
  e-books as, 161–162
  examples, 160–162
  mini-manuals as, 162
  overview of, 159–162
  passive income provided by,
    159–162
  podcasts as, 160–161
Website
  credibility influenced by, 100–104
  developing, 130

guidelines, 130
home page, 101–102
hype on, 103
as organic, 102
as real estate, 100–104
to retail buyer, 124
testimonials on, 103–104
under-construction approach to,
    102
to wholesale buyer, 124
Wholesale market
  definition of, 122
  ideal prospects in, 122–124
  retail market and, 122–124
  website to, 124
Wife, 14, 181, 199. *See also* Spouse
Wire transfers, 88
Wisdom, 148, 149
Word-of-mouth marketing, 59
Work, during vacations,
    178–179
Work location. *See* Location
Work/life balance. *See* Balance

Young, Rebecca. *See* Teskalefbre,
    Rebecca Young

Alan Weiss, PhD
President
Summit Consulting Group, Inc.
Box 1009
East Greenwich, RI 02818
Phone: 401/884–2778 Fax: 401/884–5068
Alan@summitconsulting.com
http://www.summitconsulting.com
http://www.contrarianconsulting.com
http://alansforums.com